Strategic Networks

To Arantxa

Strategic Networks

Creating the borderless organization

J. C. Jarillo

BUTTERWORTH
HEINEMANN

Butterworth-Heinemann
Linacre House, Jordan Hill, Oxford OX2 8DP
225 Wildwood Avenue, Woburn, MA 01801-2041
A division of Reed Educational and Professional Publishing Ltd

$\mathcal{R}$ A member of the Reed Elsevier plc group

OXFORD   BOSTON   JOHANNESBURG
MELBOURNE   NEW DELHI   SINGAPORE

First published 1993
Paperback edition 1995
Reprinted 1995, 1998

British Library Cataloguing in Publication Data
Jarillo, J. Carlos
    Strategic Networks: Creating the
    borderless organization
    I. Title
    658

ISBN 0 7506 2327 6

Composition by Genesis Typesetting, Laser Quay, Rochester, Kent
Printed and bound in Great Britain by MPG Books Ltd, Bodmin, Cornwall

Contents

Contents

Preface

This is an ambitious book. It tries to find a common ingredient in a number of business phenomena of great importance but whose connection is far from evident: from the current troubles of former industry leaders such as IBM or General Motors to the generalized drive to subcontracting more and more activities hitherto performed in-house; from the meteoric rise of franchising in many industries as diverse as fast-food, financial services or funeral homes to the apparently unbeatable strengths of Japanese *keiretsu*, in boom as in bust; from the current debate on whether there is any money to be made selling 'hardware', when profits really are to be found in selling 'solutions'; to the rise in importance and number of strategic alliances. All these phenomena are having a profound impact on the way business is understood in many industries, to the point where 'conventional wisdom' is being challenged almost everywhere.

But conventional wisdom is often replaced by new verities that are not necessarily more helpful than the old ones. Thus it is not uncommon to hear business experts say that some of the world industrial giants are far too integrated to be efficient. This seems well established by now. But, only a few minutes later, the same experts assert that Japanese competitors have an unfair edge because they belong to tightly integrated groups. Equally, conventional wisdom now wants IBM, DEC, and other computer manufacturers to de-emphasize their hardware business, which has turned into a 'commodity'. But Intel, maker of the microprocessors at the heart of those 'commodities', is one of the most profitable companies on earth. Simultaneously, the ultimate commodity producers, the oil companies, are fast divesting the 'value-added' businesses they entered in the last decades, to concentrate on just a few parts of their whole system. The conventional wisdom that called for 'value-added' activities and full integration has been discredited.

It is not surprising then that the last few years have seen a plethora of articles and books on topics such as networking, value-added relationships, de-layering, modularization, the need for companies to nurture long-term relationships in all spheres.[1] All those works point in one direction: companies must look at their boundaries with new eyes – things that have traditionally been 'inside' should perhaps be 'outside', and 'outsiders' might perhaps deserve the treatment of 'insiders'. But many of those articles and books just describe what seem to be 'new' practices without showing a real understanding of the underlying causes of the 'problems' and, particularly, of the long-term effects of the 'solutions'.

This simultaneous lack of satisfaction with the old accepted wisdom and lack of real understanding of the problems is thus widespread. Business people realize that the choices companies make about what part of the business to concentrate on, and how to relate to the other parts are essential, yet there is not a clear theory on how to make those choices. That theory is not evident for, as this book will show, the answers are dependent on industry characteristics, and on the way particular companies want to play the game. As a result, there is plenty of contradictory anecdotal evidence: practically every 'theory' can be supported with an example of a successful company.

It is the purpose of this book to provide the reader with a deep, rigorous understanding of why, how and when the kind of 'collaborative approach' being 'preached' by much managerial literature is the appropriate one. After all, it is crucial not to forget that companies' overarching goal is to make money, both in the short and long term. To get beyond the mere descriptive level or, what is worse, to the mere coining of new buzzwords, we have to gain a full understanding of how the different parts of a business can be coordinated in a way that is, simultaneously, efficient, flexible, and conducive to innovation. Simply telling companies to break up because large companies are unmanageable is not a very creative management solution. Nor is it enough to insist that they concentrate on the core, if we don't know how to find out what a profitable 'core' will be in five years' time. But to go beyond those platitudes will require work at the interface between economics and sociology, for the deep reasons that some organizations are more efficient than others are rooted simultaneously in both disciplines, and a partial point of view can only provide partial answers.

This book is, however, eminently readable. That has been my intent throughout, and that is what all the reviewers tell me. It is full of examples, some of them fairly detailed, so that abstract notions such as networks, transactions costs or goal congruence can be intuitively grasped.

The customary note of thanks must be relatively long, for this book has had a long genesis. The conceptual core comes from the work I did for my doctoral dissertation, now eight years ago. I studied a number of entrepreneurs, and realized that they all seemed to have an uncanny ability to get other people and companies to work for them. This led me to an attempt to conceptualize cooperation in a strict, for-profit business environment. From there I started to develop the notion of the 'strategic network' – as a set of companies that work together towards a common goal – and became interested in why such networks are in some cases more efficient than other organizations. This book is an attempt to go one step further – to explain under what circumstances this is the best way to organize a business, and how it can be done.

Evidently this long intellectual journey has left me debtor to many people. First, Howard H. Stevenson, of Harvard University, who introduced me to the topic of entrepreneurship and pushed me to develop the first insights on cooperation. Professor Joan E. Ricart, of IESE, worked with me on some of the more precise conceptualizations, visible in Chapter 6. Professor Jon I. Martínez, of Universidad A. Ibáñez has worked with me for many years now on international strategy and cooperation, and part of that work can be seen in Chapter 7. Many executives with whom I have discussed these ideas have helped me ground them in reality, providing me with a constant checking mechanism and new insights. Professors Ahmet Aykaç and Francis Bidault of IMD, and Lauris Hedaa of the Copenhagen Business School have given me timely and useful feedback. Finally my wife, Arantxa, has put up with several missed vacations, and many boring weekends, while I wrote this. I just hope it has been worthwhile.

Reference

1 For an up-to-date discussion, see John Kay, *Foundations of Corporate Success*, Oxford University Press, 1993.

Part One: Competition and Cooperation

1 A new way to compete

In 1956 a 60-year old native of Kentucky, known as Colonel Saunders, started selling to some of his friends the right to open restaurants to cook and sell a chicken dish after a Southern recipe that he had perfected in the previous twenty years. Just eight years later his amiable face, complete with goatee beard, presided over the entrance of 700 Kentucky Fried Chicken restaurants throughout the world, all selling approximately the same menu, to the same standards.

A few years later Mr Ray Krock, salesman to a milkshake machinery company, realized that there was a large potential in the ideas of one of his clients, Mr McDonald. After coming to an agreement with him, he started setting up 'franchisees' to sell the same hamburgers, made to the same rigid specifications.

Today, innumerable 'fast food chains' later, more than half the whole US restaurant market is controlled by franchise organizations, ranging from very inexpensive sandwich shops to more up-market chains specializing in seafood and full menus[1]. This dominance, which used to be a distinctive characteristic of the American market but was somewhat derided in Europe, is now spreading worldwide. That one of the largest sellers of pizza in Europe is affiliated with an American company, ultimately owned by PepsiCo, is an irony that testifies to the success of the formula.

At about the same time these 'chains' were being set up a brother and sister were starting to sell brightly coloured sweaters through a rather unconventional shop in the small town of Belluno, in a remote area north of Venice. The concept behind the merchandise and the shop proved successful, and other shops based along the same principles, sporting the same Benetton name, opened quickly in Italy, and then in

Europe. As in the case of 'fast food', the initial success of a 'chain operation' such as Benetton first led to some imitators, and then started to alter the whole way inexpensive clothing is made and sold.

Very far from Italy, in Japan, a series of companies were preparing themselves to begin seriously exporting their inexpensive automobiles to the rest of the world, starting with the American market, the largest and most open of all. Their products were not essentially different from those being made by American manufacturers: they were simply smaller and much cheaper. The difference lay in how they were made, using different manufacturing techniques. Among these techniques, one was startlingly different: the widespread use of subcontractors.

As Figure 1.1 shows, the proportion of value added by the Japanese manufacturers is much lower than that of their Western competitors, with the exception of small 'niche' producers. This has nothing to do with productivity, but with the Japanese practice of purchasing many important subsystems already finished from subcontractors. Many of the subcontractors the Japanese companies buy from, however, are not completely independent. They have exclusive supplier arrangements and even some of their equity is owned by the automobile manufacturers. These 'group' arrangements are so widespread in Japan that the American Department of Trade has complained that inter-dealings among companies within these *'keiretsu'* (groups) provide the Japanese with an 'unfair' competitive edge, for other companies cannot penetrate, in order to buy or sell, those thick webs of relationships.[2]

It is the central argument of this book that all these success stories are intimately related. Behind these successes, as behind many others I shall analyse in detail, lies a common characteristic. These successful companies do two apparently opposite things at the same time. First, they 'control' the whole production process, from raw materials to selling to the final consumer; and controlling means controlling – prices, volumes, levels of quality, working systems ... are set by the company. But, second, they do not *own* the units that provide

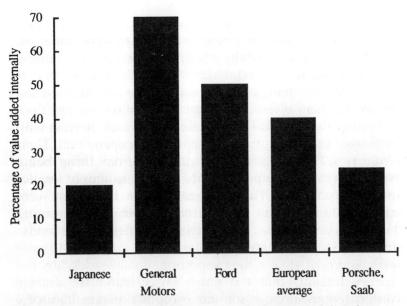

Figure 1.1 *Degree of vertical integration in the automobile industry*

them with those raw materials or subcomponents, nor the units that commercialize the finished products to the end customer. That is, these companies act simultaneously as large integrated companies, taking care of everything; and as companies that concentrate only on a few things, subcontracting the rest. As we shall see, most companies tend to do one of the two things. Few manage to do both and, in more and more circumstances, doing both is exactly the prerequisite for success.

The explanation, at its most simple, is as follows. Current competitive circumstances simultaneously demand levels of quality, low cost, innovation and fast response times that traditionally organized companies cannot deliver. By traditionally organized I mean companies that either try to make most things in-house or rely on a series of 'arm's-length' subcontractors for components or distribution. Companies that make most things in-house (called by economists vertically integrated companies) often find it hard to deliver in time, at low costs.

5

General Motors or IBM are paradigmatic. They are not only the largest and most integrated in their industries – they are also the highest cost producers. This has led to an insistence on 'restructuring' or 'modularization'.[3] But companies that do go for a narrow span of activity and 'subcontract' the rest find themselves very often cut off from innovation, fast reactions or high quality levels. This is because they lack direct contact with the final customer, or basic understanding of the underlying technologies. In any case they risk being 'sandwiched' between companies that keep the sources of innovation (subcontractors) and the sources of inspiration (distributors, those with direct contact with the customer). Moreover, coordinating hundreds of external organizations to deliver fast, cheap, and on time, is certainly not an easy task.

Yet it seems that the only way to meet the current competitive requirements, in many industries, is to 'control' a large span of all the activities that end up in a product or service, while avoiding the ills of vertically integrated companies: bureaucratization, lack of innovation, bloated costs, unresponsiveness. This feat of combining the best of both worlds is being achieved by more and more companies in more and more industries. In fact it is becoming so important that it can be said to have originated a *third way* to organize a business. That third kind of organization I call a *strategic network*. In a strategic network one company takes the role of 'central controller' and organizes the flow of goods and information among many other independent companies, making sure the final client gets exactly what he or she is supposed to get, in an efficient way.

An example is given by a chain such as McDonald's. From a point of view of *organization*, McDonald's acts as a vertically integrated company: it decides even the potato seeds that will be used to raise the raw materials for its fries worldwide. It also decides things as removed in the 'business chain' as the cap to be worn by salespeople or, within legal bounds, the final retail price of all its products. But these are not McDonald's' products! The company does not own the producers of raw materials, it (in most cases) does not own the restaurants, nor the makers of the specialized equipment crucial to ensuring quality and success. From the point of view of *ownership*, McDonald's is not an integrated company. But, of course, one cannot really conceive of McDonald's without its franchisees and its closely tied suppliers: *the essence of McDonald's is its 'system'.* Thus the whole system has to be considered together, for it acts together.

This is a strategic network: an arrangement by which companies set up a web of close relationships that form a veritable *system* geared to providing product of services in a coordinated way. These networks are becoming dominant in more and more industries, and the reason is that they can meet the current competitive requirements better than old ways of organizing economic activity.

Current competitive requirements

It can probably be said that competition has always been strong. But the current widespread comments about the special intensity of competition are clearly warranted. The speed at which change is happening in the business world is certainly accelerating, because the impact of technology is a cumulative one: every improvement in information technology, in transportation systems, in management systems builds upon the previous ones, thus generating an exponential rate of growth. Figure 1.2 shows different time-lags between scientific innovation and its commercial application.

Another example is provided by the shortening development time in the automobile industry, as shown in Figure 1.3. These examples point in one direction: it is more and more frequent that even successful companies cannot sit back for a while and catch their breath. They must be innovating all the time, facing constant pressure from competitors to do so faster.

This quickening pace of innovation has been accompanied by a generalized drop in prices. Thus companies must cut their costs constantly, finding new ways to produce, trying to work smarter, not harder; and, to compound these two

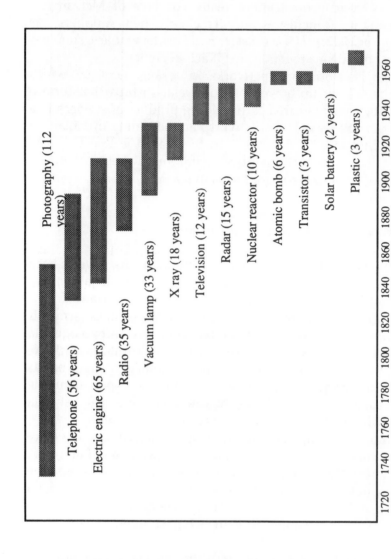

Figure 1.2 *Time from scientific discovery to market innovation*

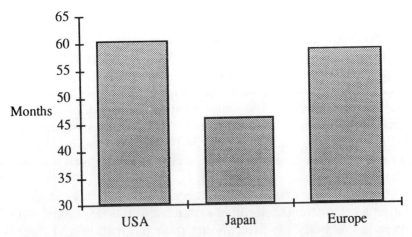

Figure 1.3 *Shortening development times in the automobile industry*

problems, quality expectations have been raised in most industries. What used to be 'good enough' in now simply unacceptable. 'Zero-defect quality' is a level aimed at by more and more companies.

Most (not all) of these pressures stem from the single most important economic development of the past forty years: the globalization of competition. The entry of US multinationals into Europe provoked a 'revolution' similar to the entry of Japanese products into the US.[4] The old competitive *status quo* was suddenly shattered, and companies had to adjust to the newcomers, to decide to buck past trends. Today dozens of countries are trying to enter the world economic stage at once, bringing such low costs and strong determination as no established, 'developed' company could have imagined 20 years ago.

Organization as a way to meet strategic demands

All these pressures, which have just started, call for two characteristics in companies wanting to succeed. *Efficiency* to deliver better and better products at lower costs, and *flexibility* to do so in always different ways, learning constantly to do things differently and to do different things. Most companies under competitive pressure try desperately to cut costs, only to realize that this seriously impairs their ability to innovate. The only solution is to adopt radical change: companies must organize themselves in radically different ways, and grow beyond their current organizational constraints, for the way a company organizes itself has a huge impact on its results.

Organization drives performance because it lays down, among other things, incentive systems and the ways in which people interact, thus determining their motivation and their ability to learn, to develop new, creative ways of doing things. Different strategic goals require different organizational characteristics, and the organization that is better suited to the specific strategic needs of its time and its industry wins out. That is why, in many mature industries, one finds a remarkable organizational similarity among competitors: over the years, they have all converged on the 'ideal' organization for their business. In this sense one can think of the introduction of organizational forms as a sort of Darwinian process: over time, new forms emerge, in this case thanks to the creativity of people (or just by chance), not to some genetic alteration. Most of these new ideas never get very far or, if they do, are dependent on the personal characteristics of the organizer, and cannot be transferred. But, from time to time, one sees new forms that are both clearly superior in terms of performance *and* transferable. These forms become the 'accepted way to do business'. Competitors either adopt the new form or disappear in front of the better organized companies.

The functional organization that informed practically every business up to the Second World War was, over time, increasingly supplanted by the divisional organization, where a company that competes in several businesses 'cuts across' functional lines to create full divisions, with their own functions. After General Motors and Du Pont 'invented' the divisional form, it was just a matter of time before all large corporations adopted it, for it was a clearly superior way of meeting the different competitive requirements that these large, diversified companies were facing, i.e. how to maintain a business focus inside what had become a huge, unresponsive, and more and more unspecialized bureaucracy.[5] Interestingly enough, the traditional functional organization is still the most efficient way to organize most small and medium-sized companies, and those that have imitated the large ones by adopting the divisional organization have suffered as a result, and have gone back to the simpler forms – or died under their self-inflicted inefficiency.

The idea of arranging organizational activities around the business (something relatively external) as opposed to the functions (internal) better to meet competitive demands has kept progressing, and companies have taken further steps such as product managers, key client accounts, even activity-based costing, which is a way to break down the functional organization into what the company really does from the point of view of customers. Once an organization innovation proves its superiority, it is always adopted. Thus one can see that practically all professional service firms (accounting, consulting, law) are organized as partnerships; that all investment banks were partnerships, until they decided to go to the capital markets; that most consumer goods companies are organized along product management lines; etc. There may indeed be a component of imitation in that similarity, but there is no question that some ways to organize a company are better to meet some strategic requirements than others, and the superior forms are quickly adopted in a competitive environment.

The central thesis of this book is that the strategic network is such an organizational innovation, and that it is winning over in more and more industries, because it is able to capture the main advantages of two organizations considered mutually exclusive, so exclusive that, in fact, they can be conceived as the two different ways of organizing any economic transaction. By capturing that uniquely new set of advantages, this form of organization can respond better to a uniquely new set of competitive pressures.

11

The two basic ways to organize economic activity: vertical integration and subcontracting

Practically any economic activity requires sub-activities: in order to produce and sell a car, somebody has to perform a huge number of operations, from the design of the car, to the design of thousands of individual parts, the production and delivery of those parts, the assembly, the market promotion, etc. Obviously each of these activities has to be coordinated with the rest: only so many parts are needed, and they must be of a specific kind, delivered at a specific date and location, for instance. This task of coordination is absolutely impressive, if one stops to think about it. To continue with the example of a car, thousands of different pieces, most of them model-specific, have to be assembled in a rigid sequence, in a matter of a few hours (only fifteen in the case of the most efficient manufacturers). It does not take an expert in the automobile industry to realize that it is precisely the *coordination* of the whole system, between design and manufacturing, between parts delivery and assembly, between assembly and sales, that determines the ultimate competitiveness of each individual company.

A traditional, managerial way to make sure there is coordination among those disparate activities is to put somebody in charge of them; if it is the same company that engages in those activities, a coordinating authority can be introduced that will make sure that every part of the system works to a common end, in a harmonic way. This was, indeed, Henry Ford's way of organizing his business: once the assembly line was in place, and the pace of assembly greatly facilitated by the interchangeability of parts, it was absolutely essential that parts were indeed interchangeable (quality concern) and that they were delivered on time, at a low cost (reliability concern).

To assure that, Ford simply set up the whole operation by himself, from steelmaking to the ultimate assembly operations, for he couldn't find suppliers who would deliver to the unusually high standards that his strategy required. Moreover, his strong management ability allowed him to organize

12

thousands of unskilled immigrant workers into a 'machine' delivering the most reliable, lowest cost automobiles ever manufactured. This way to organize the whole system, from raw materials to the final customer (or, at least, parts of the system) became known as *vertical integration* – one company integrates within its boundaries many or even most of the activities needed to deliver the final product or service.

In the last 75 years vertical integration has become the standard way to organize most large businesses, whether industrial or service-oriented. For instance, most banks will take care of the whole cycle, from taking deposits (in branches they own, by employees they employ) to recycling them into loans to individuals or companies, while keeping track of all the underlying transactions in their own computers, attended by their own systems employees. It is in this respect that vertical integration has, in a majority of industries, become the *dominant organizational form*, along the lines discussed in these pages.

Things could, theoretically, be organized differently: Ford's could buy steel from a steelmaker, have the parts manufactured and delivered by a third party, get the designs from a specialized outfit, and so on. In fact, it could conceivably not even assemble cars; it could choose just to market the cars, and subcontract the rest. After all, this is what a successful 'manufacturer' of sporting shoes such as Nike does: the firm never *makes* a shoe, just markets them, and seem to be fairly successful at that. Henry Ford felt this was not best for his company, but many other business people strongly believe a dis-integrated company to be better for them.

Subcontracting is essentially a *second organizational form*, market based: when a company needs an input, it goes to the market and has it delivered by an external party. When we look at the whole system that delivers Nike shoes, for instance, we don't see, as in the case of Ford's, a large bureaucracy planning in detail and telling everybody what to do. Rather, we find a 'constellation' of companies, from large chemical manufacturers that make the soles, to smaller operations in the Far East that sew the different parts.[6] If we look 'downstream', that is, towards the final customer, we find something similar: the distribution channel is multi-layered, with importing companies, wholesalers and retailers, none of which are Nike-owned or controlled. Thus this second organizational form, called subcontracting or market-based, not only refers to the non-ownership of suppliers, it also refers to the non-integration of those intermediate steps between the company and the customer. In an extreme case a market-based industrial organization would consist of a series of companies each specializing in only one activity.

These two organizational forms are not 'pure', in the sense that every vertically integrated company ends up buying some inputs outside and, in many cases, using external distribution mechanisms; and there are very few (if any) companies that do only one thing, buying all their inputs in the open market, and selling in it all their outputs. There is, nevertheless, a clear tendency to group more or less activities within the same company.

Like any other organizational form, these two affect results: if the coordination of the different activities needed to deliver a final product or service is an important source of competitive advantage, then that form which ends up coordinating those activities better will be adopted by more and more companies. The company with the best components, delivered on time, for instance, will end up winning over the company that only gets overpriced components, and has to buy them in large batches, because it cannot ensure smooth delivery. It is now clear that the choice of organizational form (vertical integration versus market-based subcontracting) has a clear impact in the final outcome. Thus there are two kinds of costs or sources of value: *doing* the things, i.e. the different activities needed to deliver a finished product or service, and *coordinating* those activities. This second set of costs (and sometimes the first) is directly affected by the choice of organizational form.

This choice is changing fast. As mentioned before, vertical integration has been the preferred organization for many years in many industries dominated by large companies, but its many problems have prompted a strong move towards the second, market-based form. Many companies have realized that by integrating a large number of very different activities, they were actually losing focus, developing rigidities, and finding it more and more difficult to coordinate in a time- and cost-efficient fashion. Thus 'restructuring', so widespread in many industries in the 1980s, has essentially meant de-integrating so-called 'non core' activities, in an effort to focus the company on only some aspects, leaving to the market mechanisms the task of ensuring adequate supplies and distribution outlets.

But, as vertical integration has some problems (essentially suffocating bureaucracy, and the possibility of having units whose costs are out of line with their real competitive position) that become only apparent after a number of years, so subcontracting has its risks. Many companies are realizing that, if they subcontract their inputs, they may be letting the basic technological knowledge, on which their business is ultimately based, go to their subcontractors; that, by selling only to a few intermediate customers, far removed from the final user, they lose touch with market realities; or that, after all, coordinating a large number of outsiders is not an easy task anyway, and long-term costs, including lack of time responsiveness, end by going up. Thus subcontracting may seem a very efficient short-term solution, but it may develop some very serious problems over time.

A company that adopts the market-based organization tends to look for multiple suppliers and customers, to avoid becoming hostage to any one of them (who would want to have one client or one supplier?). But this forces the company into significant purchasing and marketing expenses (gathering information on suppliers, supplying information to customers), and prevents it from making specific investments in any one relationship. This is fine, as long as those specific investments (machinery, technology, etc.) don't give a competitor a clear efficiency edge. In a way the plight of many companies that don't want to invest in training, although it would increase their productivity, because they fear their employees would leave them once trained, is an extreme case of the problem of arm's-length relationships: they force a short-term logic, which is not the most efficient in many

15

businesses, where decisions only reveal their full impact over time.

If, to be safe, a company has to keep a variety of suppliers, it cannot possibly ask for very specific solutions from them, and it thus becomes less efficient than it could conceivably be; if it has to keep a large customer base, it may not be able to afford to tailor its products to too many clients, except at the price of another efficiency penalty. The immediate solution, to reduce the number of relationships, would put the company in a delicate position, depending on a few suppliers or clients for key, specific, parts of its business. This is a risky position, one that many business people have traditionally tried to avoid, whether by integrating vertically or by paying the efficiency penalty.

The emerging way: strategic networks

If there was an organizational form that could provide companies with the advantages of the two old organizations, it would clearly become a superior form. Think of an organization that would provide companies with the long-term planning security of a large, integrated company, where one can invest in the relationships because they are intrinsically stable. It would provide the company with the advantages inherent to being in direct contact with the customer and the technology, thus being able to innovate faster than de-integrated companies. But, at the same time, it would do away with the coordinating bureaucracy, keep the entrepreneurial drive of independent firms, and make sure that the unit performing each activity was perfectly well adapted to that activity, not to an 'overall way' of doing business.

That organization, for instance, would be able to come up with outstanding technological breakthroughs, because the hottest scientists around would want to work for it, and there would be an atmosphere of technological achievement, together with direct financial rewards for them, as in a small high-tech company. Those assembly operations that require no special machinery or expertise would be carried out in small units, where the manager has all the motivation of the owner, and efficiency is achieved by doing away with bureaucracy, supervision and 'big company' overheads. Activities that require a large scale to be performed efficiently would, however, be performed at such scale, such as purchasing, machine-based assembly, market research, etc. Throughout, coordination costs would be minimized: each unit, by working for its own interest, would act in the benefit of the group, without imposing the burden of a controlling, reward-awarding bureaucracy.

Sounds fancy? Think of McDonald's. Technology is developed on the basis of the huge economies of scale provided by a chain of thousands of restaurants worldwide. Similarly, advertising is efficiently done through television. But, as is essential in a service operation, the owner of the restaurant is never far away. Most McDonald restaurants do not belong to McDonald's, and thus they keep all their entrepreneurial efficiency. But they *do* 'belong': there is a common image, technology, consistency, etc. The relationship of each restaurant owner with McDonald's is, in terms of developing specific investments, closer to that of a subsidiary than that of an independent agent: there is plenty of investment from the franchisee in McDonald's (the franchise fee, the learning that is company-specific) and from McDonald's in the franchisee (exclusive rights to a territory, abundant training). But these cross-investments do not diminish the advantages of independence.

In this respect, it is interesting to note that, in most franchise chains, the restaurants owned by the chain are less profitable than those franchised to outsiders,[7] even taking into account that some of the company-owned operations are used as training ground for managers. If the technology and basic operations are the same, then the motivation of individual ownership must make the difference. It is that motivation, which only comes with small companies, plus the advantages of technology and marketing clout, which come with large companes, that forms a clearly superior combination. This is a strategic network, and the advantages it offers are taking over more and more companies in more and more industries.

Description of this book

In the next chapters I intend to analyse very carefully those advantages, and show when and how they can be obtained. To do that with the necessary rigour, I will start by studying in detail a concept that I have used implicitly in this chapter without actually defining it: the business system. It means essentially the collection of all the activities that have to be performed in order to deliver a product or service to a final customer. As we have seen, it is precisely the different ways to organize the system, i.e. to coordinate the different steps along it, that is the focus of this study, for it is central to this book's main argument that on that choice hangs a great deal of any company's long-term competitiveness. Studying the business system in detail will let us understand why some of its activities are more profitable than others, both in the short and long term; it will be the necessary groundwork for the whole book. To introduce the basic concepts of business systems analysis I discuss the computer industry in detail, showing how the proposed framework can help one understand not only the present, apparently confusing situation, but also its genesis and probable evolution.

Part Two of the book is concerned with the different ways to organize the business system for maximum efficiency and flexibility. Chapter 3 studies vertical integration, which provides the company with the advantage of having those activities of the business system considered important under the same managerial umbrella, thus saving on coordination costs. It also prevents suppliers from 'stealing' at least part of the company's competitive advantages. But in many cases vertical integration does not come free. Coordinating things inside a company does also have costs, in the shape of bureaucracy, technological rigidities, lack of focus, and 'spill-over effects': the more profitable parts of the company end up subsidizing inefficient ways of doing business in those parts that could not, on their own, afford such luxuries. All these problems, which tend to take some time to show up, have led in the last decade to countless restructurings.

Chapter 4 deals with subcontracting, which is of course the proposed solution to the problems just discussed. But the study of the domestic appliance industry shows how subcontractors can end up usurping the original manufacturers' competitive advantages, to the point of driving them out of business. The chapter then describes the steps that the Western automobile manufacturers took to prevent that from happening. They succeeded, but introduced so many systemic costs that new competitors, with a fresh approach, could displace them in a relatively short period of time. Thus subcontracting, sometimes presented as the panacea to the large company's ills, has its serious drawbacks too.

Chapter 5 introduces in full view the third way to organize the business system: the strategic network. To do it, I describe in detail Benetton, a company that has set up such a network. The discussion tries to show how a company can enter a very mature industry and obtain an extremely solid (and sustainable) competitive position. It appears that Benetton's competitive advantage lies in the superior way it has organized its business, more than in any specific way of performing parts of it. The fact that many in the industry are imitating Benetton's organization with excellent results is a clear indication that Benetton's success is at least partially due to its superior organizational efficiency, not just to the creative genius of its founder.

Part Three of the book is entitled 'How to step up and manage a strategic network'. In Chapter 6 an attempt is made to establish a general theory of strategic networks, so that its core characteristics can be understood, as a first step to applying the model to other industries. An effort is made to show under what circumstances a strategic network is indeed the best way to organize a system, and what are the necessary characteristics that the different relationships must have for the network to be successful (generate superior profits system-wide) and stable (by distributing those profits in a way that makes participants in the network want to stay).

Finally, I discuss the managerial implications for managing a network, or managing in a network, which are different in some crucial respects from managing a 'stand alone' company.

Chapter 7 expands the concepts of networking and cooperation to the area of international strategy, where they are highly relevant: strategic networks have become an extremely efficient way to internationalize a company, capturing many of the advantages of multinational operations, without many of their costs. Finally, Chapter 8 tries to put the main ideas discussed in the book into perspective, summarizing the key points, and discussing further areas for development. A bibliography for the reader interested in deepening his understanding of the book's topic is then added.

References

1 'How to succeed at cloning a small business', *Fortune*, 28 October 1985.
2 See, for instance, 'Congress draws bead on *keiretsu* practices', *Automotive News*, 21 October 1991.
3 See 'The modular corporation', by Shawn Tully, *Fortune*, 8 February 1993.
4 Those worried about the 'predatory' competitiveness of Japanes companies should remember J.J. Servan-Schreiber's influential book, *The American Challenge*, published in 1965, where the terrifying enemy was the US multinational, intrinsically superior in its business methods to the European companies.
5 For a detailed account of the shift from functional to divisional structures, see Chandler, Alfred, *Strategy and Structure: Chapters in the History of the American Industrial Enterprise*, Cambridge, Mass.: The MIT Press, 1962.
6 See Lorenzoni, Gianni, 'From Vertical Integration to Vertical Disintegration', paper presented at the Strategic Management Society Conference, Montreal, 1982.
7 See Shelton, John, 'Allocative Efficiency vs X-Efficiency: Comment'", *American Economic Review*, vol. 57, 1967.

2 Understanding the playing field: the business system

As outlined in the previous chapter, the ambitious goal of this book is to show how a different way to organize relationships among companies can result in a consistently superior business performance in specific industries. To do that with the necessary level of rigour to make it useful, I must provide the reader with an understanding of what the constituent parts of an industry are. To understand correctly this level of disaggregation is essential, for the very argument of this book is that, by rearranging those primary elements of industries, superior performance can be achieved. It is necessary therefore, to devote this chapter to the study of those basic elements that constitute economic life.

Since the beginning of strategic thinking, the individual company was the unit of analysis.[1] This makes sense, for it is to meet the needs of business managers, in charge of individual companies, that strategic concepts were developed. Thus the first ideas tried to help managers align their company with its environment, talking about opportunities and threats, strengths and weaknesses.[2]

Helpful as this was, it left many questions unanswered. For example, what is really a strength? In a competitive world it is difficult to judge anything on absolute terms, without referring it to competitors. Thus came the consideration of whole industries as units of analysis: one had to understand the *structural characteristics* of, say, the automobile industry, before actually knowing whether large size, for instance, was a strength or a weakness.[3] This was a very important step forward, for it provided a rigorous methodology to carry out the 'SWOT' (strengths, weaknesses, opportunities, and threats) analysis recommended by the early strategic writers.

The structural analysis of industries as it has been popularized, particularly in the work of Michael Porter, has one important shortcoming, however. It considers 'industries' as 'black boxes': lumps of economic activity, made up by a number of competitors, outlined by their suppliers and customers.[4] This view did provide some analytical thoughts on how relations between the industry and its suppliers and buyers would go, but it did not provide an encompassing view of industries as including all major players, from raw materials to the final consumer.[5] And that is what we need: a way to understand the whole economic activity that ends up in a good or service, to distinguish its constituent parts, to understand why some parts are more profitable than others and, finally, why value can be created by coordinating those parts differently. For it is clear that many of the basic concepts of competitive strategy used today, such as economies of scale, barriers to entry, differentiation, etc., apply very differently to different parts of a company.[6] Thus the company is both too small and too large a unit of analysis. It is too large because most relevant strategic concepts apply differently to its different parts. It is too small because ultimate strategic success cannot be understood in isolation. We must then take whole industries, and then break them down, not into the companies that make them up but into the economic activities that end up producing the product or service. Since companies decide which activities to engage in, and those decisions vary, they are not a homogeneous, comparable set. Only activities can be studied directly in a first analysis.

The business system[7]

Take the relation between manufacturing and retailing. One way to look at it is that of a zero-sum game: the higher the manufacturer's margins, the lower those that go the retailer, and vice-versa. Thus, in competitive terms, it is clear that the profits of one side are determined, at least partially, by its ability to defend them against the other. That is what a zero-sum game means: what a party wins is at the expense of the other, so the net gain is always zero. But, at the same time, the more innovations the manufacturers introduce, the brisker sales will be at the retail level. Conversely, the better retailers become at distributing, the higher the sales will be for the manufacturers. The relation is obviously a complex one, and no simplistic view can be taken: retailers are not, in principle, either 'the enemy' or 'the ally'. They may be either both, or none of the above. In fact, they may be even the same thing, if a given company both manufactures and retails.

Evidently something symmetrical could be said of suppliers: there are so many examples of suppliers providing creative solutions to a company's problems that is hard to see them just as providers of inputs whose cost has to be minimized. Thus no complete analysis can be performed on either side without simultaneously analysing the other, and the different ways both sides can relate to each other. That is one reason why we have to look at the whole industry, to understand how superior performance can actually be achieved, without being constrained by companies' borders, which are arbitrary. The other reason is that what matters in the end to all participants in the system is the competitiveness of the final product, and how each activity relates to the others does affect that competitiveness, as we shall see.

We shall do that by analysing in some detail the computer industry. In many ways it is a convenient example: the industry is at the same time concentrated (a few manufacturers are large and well known) and diverse (there are many different players in it); it is fast moving, so the impact of strategic decisions can quickly be grasped; and its products and many of its protagonists are surely known to most readers of this book.

Much has gone on before we are able to buy a personal computer. It has to be designed, its components purchased and assembled after they have been designed and made, the final product distributed to wholesalers, retailers, (or directly to the customer), and it will probably be advertised. The basic software that drives the machine (at least, the operating system) must be written, somehow printed (normally on diskettes and chips) and installed in the computer. Only then can a personal computer be bought by a final user.

Figure 2.1 represents these main steps. All companies performing those steps are what constitute, for our purposes, the 'personal computer industry'. Observe that this definition is vague: many people would restrict membership in the industry to 'computer makers'. But the dynamics of the business cannot be understood without looking at all the components of the chain in Figure 2.1, and this is the approach I will take.

The crucial point is that, for the purpose of our analysis, the industry is composed not of the *companies* taking part in it, but of the *activities* necessary to deliver the product or service. Evidently those activities will be carried out by companies (although universities may perform basic research and government monopolies can play a role in distribution). In fact most companies perform activities that are part of different industries, and it is difficult to find two companies performing exactly the same activities. One of the basic strategic decisions for a company, as we shall see, is to choose what exactly are the activities it is going to perform. But the activity is the basic building block of industries: it is at the activity level that much of the competitive advantage – driver of profits – can be gained.

It is then important to distinguish between a given economic activity and the company that performs it. Compare two conspicuous players in the microcomputer industry, IBM and Dell. IBM needs no introduction. Dell is an extremely successful American marketer of IBM-compatible personal computers. It is clear that, in Figure 2.1, they do not occupy the same boxes, i.e. they don't perform the same activities.

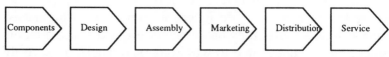

Figure 2.1 *Business system of the computer industry*

IBM designs many components, manufactures them, designs the computer, assembles it, and delivers it though a complex, multi-tiered distribution system, accompanied in many cases of its own, proprietary basic software. Dell, on its part, simply gathers components (including software) and assembles them, following a design that simply tries to imitate IBM's as closely as legally possible. In this sense it performs far fewer steps than IBM to the final production and sale of a personal computer. On the other hand, it performs two key activities in-house: it sells directly, on the phone, to its customers, and it provides them with after-sales service, for it does not have dealers, contrary to practically every other company in the business (see Figure 2.2). Thus companies can very much decide what activities they want to perform and what activities they leave to what become their suppliers or their customers. Choosing the activities the company is to carry on its own (which I will call the *configuration* of the company) is evidently essential to its success, as we shall see.

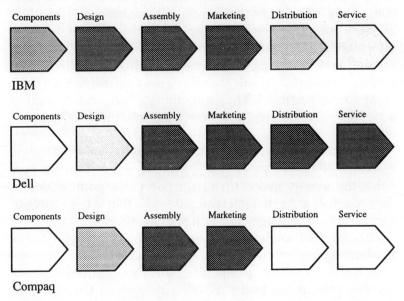

Figure 2.2 *Activities performed directly by three personal computer vendors*

One last point has to be made in this description of the business system. What exactly is an *activity*? One can in fact take the level of aggregation way down. Manufacturing, for instance, encompasses many things, from design of the manufacturing processes to the training of manufacturing employees. Where shall we draw the line? Two criteria matter: the first is that the activity can stand on its own, i.e. conceivably an independent company could carry it as its only activity. In this respect training might be considered an independent activity, in as much as it need not be tied to actual manufacturing, for a third party could provide the training, as happens indeed in some industries, where mixed associations of government and business set up training schemes to make a particular segment of the workforce more 'employable'. As the reader will have quickly noticed, this is a highly subjective judgement. In fact a typical source of new business ideas, as I will explain in Chapter 4, is to spot an activity that was always done as part of a larger one, and sell it on its own. A good example, in the computer industry, is a service called 'facilities management', by which a company completely takes over the computer department of another, taking care of everything, just delivering, for a fee, the information the client wants, and freeing it of all the hassles of owning and operating something as highly specialized (and perhaps removed from the client's basic business) as a computer department. Thus something as imbedded in other activities as 'managing' can be turned into an activity on its own.

The second criterion is that the activity have 'strategic relevance'. This relevance may be due to one of two reasons: either the activity makes up a large part of the value added in the industry, or its characteristics are such that it is a source of competitive advantage, as I will analyse shortly.

This kind of analysis will then yield a map with fuzzy borders: since, by definition, every activity can be sub-contracted to other companies, all those subcontractors become part of the industry. What matters in the end is to draw a map that captures all the important steps that are required to satisfy a given customer need. Of course some

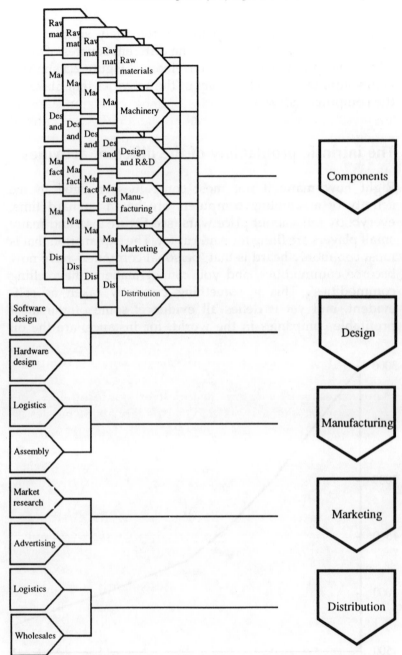

Figure 2.3 *A slightly more expanded view of the computer industry's business system*

industries will have a map that is relatively simpler than others. But it essential to isolate the different sources of value added and profit, and their interrelations. Figure 2.3 shows a (still simplified but richer) map of the activities that make up the computer industry.

The intrinsic profitability of the different activities

Right now many if not most companies engaged in the activity of assembling computers are having a hard time: everybody talks about price wars (see Figure 2.4), and many small players are filing for bankruptcy. The explanation that is most commonly heard is that 'personal computers have now become commodities, and you cannot make money selling commodities'. This is something currently taken as self-evident, and yet it defies all evidence: some of the most profitable companies in the world, for instance, are the oil

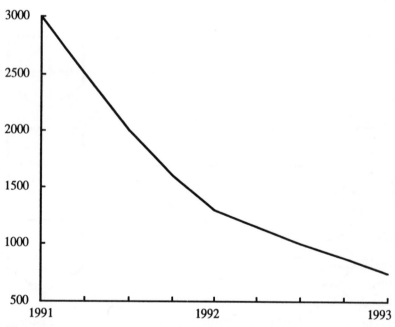

Figure 2.4 *Drop in prices in personal computers*

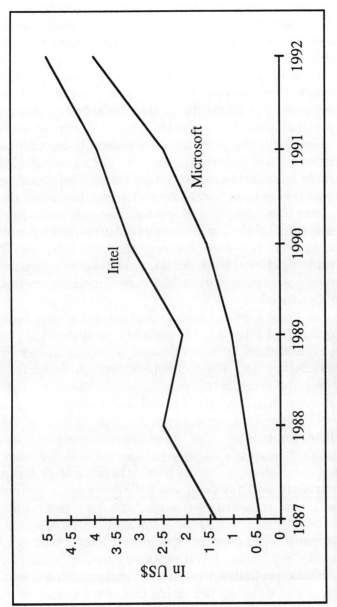

Figure 2.5 *Earnings per share at Microsoft and Intel*

companies, which do very little but extract, elaborate, and sell the ultimate commodity. Most of their attempts to get into activities with higher 'value added' (the supposed solution to computer manufacturers' problems) have been less than profitable.

But there is more. While computer assemblers file for bankruptcy, two conspicuous players in the industry, Intel and Microsoft, one on the 'hard' side, the other on the 'soft', are experiencing record results (Figure 2.5). For those readers not familiar with the industry, let me simply say that Intel manufactures the microprocessors at the heart of IBM-compatible, standard personal computers, and Microsoft sells the operating system, or basic software, that runs those computers. If a computer does not have an Intel micro-processor (or a 'clone') and a copy of Microsoft's operating system, it cannot run the software programs written for IBM-compatible machines. Understanding why some activities in the system are more profitable than others is therefore absolutely crucial.

The first thing we must realize (and it is often forgotten) is that the different activities that make up the system are really different businesses, in many crucial ways, no matter how interrelated they are. The technology tends to be different, and with it the potential for profits.

What does that potential depend on? It depends on the ability of companies to do something unique or do it at lower costs than competitors, and do so on a sustainable basis. Companies making the microprocessor that is at the heart of personal computers can make money because their designs are proprietary, and any company willing to offer a computer that will run standard software must pay Intel for its components. This is because Intel's design can be patented. If any company could copy Intel's designs, Intel would not be particularly profitable, for competitors would push prices down. Intel's profitability is not in 'making' chips, but in creating designs that go into chips that other manufacturers 'need' to buy from them in order to sell their assembled machines. Put another way, the reason customers buy Intel processors is obviously their performance: they can run IBM-compatible software. That does not depend on how they are manufactured, but on how they are designed.

Manufacturing may or may not be a source of competitive advantage (of profits). It would be one if it could be performed in a way that was clearly superior to competitors' on a consistent basis; and this today is not the case for standard semiconductor manufacturing, which several dozen companies in the world can do with comparable competence. Thus it is conceivable that Intel could completely subcontract its manufacturing and it would still be profitable. In fact Intel does some contracting: it licenses its designs to other manufacturers, because its customers like to have a 'second source'. Although the terms of those licences tend to remain private, it is not hard to imagine who captures most of the value added in the manufacture and sale of those components made by Intel's licensees.

Interestingly, Intel's profitability has become so high that some companies have, at great cost, 'reverse-engineered' their microprocessors, and are selling them at lower prices than those made by Intel. Thus Intel now finds a real limit to its monopoly ability to raise prices. Predictably, its answer is three-pronged: faster development cycles for new designs (thus leaving less time for competitors to copy them); legal actions to deter copying; and advertising its brand name to the final users, trying to persuade them that better computers have 'Intel inside', as opposed to a (functionally equivalent) processor made by any competitor. All three have a cost, which shows the limits of the value added that Intel can capture, i.e. how 'protected' its activity really is.

This takes us to the interesting point of trying to define 'value added'. We can go back to the personal computer industry map and add the average proportion of the retail sale that is taken by each step, as shown in Figure 2.6. According to this, one of the activities that adds the largest amount of value is distribution, and yet many traditional computer retailers are going out of business. This is because it is one thing is to add value, and a very different thing to capture part of that value as profit margins. Thus an activity may cost a lot and yield low profits, and vice versa:

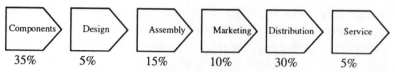

Components	Design	Assembly	Marketing	Distribution	Service
35%	5%	15%	10%	30%	5%

Figure 2.6   *Value added through the system*

Microsoft's proportion of value added over a total micro-computer is very small (less than 5 per cent), yet it is a hugely profitable company, because whoever wants to use an IBM-compatible computer must buy Microsoft's proprietary (and inexpensive) operating system. Again, the example of Intel is clarifying: Intel captures a large proportion of the value included in a microprocessor, *whether it actually makes it or it is made by one of its licensees.* The intrinsically profitable activity therefore is not to manufacture (or even less distribute) microprocessors, but to design them, provided that both the design is patentable and that it is somehow needed by purchasers (it is the industry standard).

Thus when business people talk of activities with more or less value added, they are actually referring to activities with better or worse margins; and those margins depend, as we have seen, on the possibility of developing the activity in a unique way, be it because the basic design is protectable by patents, or because companies performing the activity can do so in a way that permits them to obtain lower costs than competitors on a sustainable basis. These two 'generic ways' of capturing value added have been discussed at length in the strategic literature of the last years, and have even given rise to a discussion on whether they are mutually exclusive or not. They clearly are not. In the next few pages I shall review some of the basic reasons why some activities are intrinsically more profitable than others.

The first set of reasons is that the company performing the activity may not be easily replaced by another one (be it a competitor or the customer itself), because it is impossible to repeat what the company does, at least within a reasonable cost. We have seen that it is the *patentability* of Intel's microprocessor designs that brings in the profit: whichever company attains a status of 'industry standard setter' will make money, for customers will need microprocessors that work to that standard, and the legal system makes sure that only the inventor (and the licensees) can deliver them. It is a situation very similar to Microsoft's: there are dozens of companies in the world that can write a software package that would be functionally equivalent to its operating system, but to make it exactly compatible (so that programs written for Microsoft's systems would run on them, which is absolutely essential if the new system were to sell) would be either much too expensive or illegal, because computer code is defended by copyright laws.

Note, then, that this condition for profitability (that things be patentable) depends on the very nature of the activity: software designs are largely patentable, for example, but box styles are not. Thus, to a large extent, the attractiveness of the activity (its potential for profits) depends on the activity itself, not on the will of the companies engaged in it (although their behaviour will obviously be important in enforcing it). This is why books on strategy refer to intrinsic profitability as 'structural', i.e. depending on the technological characteristics of the business (activity), not of the companies engaged in it. Again, microprocessor are patentable (and thus potentially profitable) because our laws so want it; automobile styling is not patentable for the same reason. Companies in the business simply take advantage of these structural characteristics or, at most, try to influence them (through lobbying). But the *real* source of profits (the protectability of the designs) lies outside the companies, in the nature of the activities.

There are other reasons why a company may not be able to substitute for another when performing a given profitable activity, even if there are no patents or copyrights to worry about. One of them, of extreme importance in the history of the computer industry, is the existence of switching costs.

For any user of a large computer installation, the investment in software (programs tailor-made to suit the company's specific requirements such as pay-roll processing, invoicing, management information systems) becomes, over the years, much larger than the investment in hardware. When the time comes to renew the machines, because they have become obsolete or the company has simply outgrown them, the company finds itself 'forced' to buy a machine that will run its existing software, for doing otherwise would imply a huge expenditure in rewriting the software. If the different manufacturers use essentially incompatible systems, they make sure that their customers will stay with them forever: competitors cannot snatch them away, because of the huge switching cost faced by the buyer. This makes selling computers based on a proprietary system, i.e. on a system that makes sure that only computers of that maker will run the customer's software, potentially a hugely profitable business, as IBM has shown over many years.[8]

Of course customers may not be entirely happy with the situation, and, as soon as microcomputers appear with common ('open', in industry slang) systems, they go straight for them, dumping the larger machines as soon as technology makes it feasible. The fact that users of IBM microcomputers can dump them and buy a Dell (or a Compaq, an Acer, or any of the other 200 brands), and maintain all their investment in software and training necessarily lowers the potential margins of selling microcomputers, compared to selling computers based on proprietary systems. In this simple fact, plus the extreme difficulty of changing the workings of a company used to huge margins, lies the root of IBM's present (and future) troubles.

Switching costs appear in many activities, and are frequently sought by suppliers of course. There is the old saying about giving away the razor and then charging for the blades (if any blades would do, the idea would be a bad one). If the activity is of such a nature that it demands an independent investment by the customer (software, training), and that investment cannot be applied to the product (or service) sold by another supplier, there is a switching cost. Thus many people have kept on buying Lotus's 1–2–3 spreadsheet program, at a fairly high price, when many software companies could supply a functionally equivalent product, at a much lower price. But anybody who has mastered such a program knows the amount of hours and effort involved in mastering its 'commands': once that investment is made, nobody is going to buy another spreadsheet to save £200 and then spend the best of two weeks working to master it.[9]

In fact switching costs may become so important that governments feel they must step in. Thus the European Commission has imposed heavy fines on Tetra-Pak for, among other things, its practice of demanding that users of its liquid-packing equipment use only paperboard provided by Tetra-Pak. A client trying to get that important raw material somewhere else would have to buy new machinery.[10]

There are many other activities than can be performed, at least from the customer's point of view, in a unique way, thus making them potentially profitable. The old (really old, now) saying among data processing professionals that 'nobody ever got fired for buying IBM' exemplifies an interesting source of profitability – reputation.

In many instances buying a large computer is not really buying a computer in the same sense as buying a car. What the client wants is not a machine but the solution to an information problem that the customer himself may not be able to define clearly, let alone solve. Thus some consulting is needed before actually deciding which machines and software the customer really needs. In a situation where customers do not really know what they need, it makes sense to stick to a prestigious supplier, who will deliver, be it only to protect its reputation. Certainly competitors may offer functionally equivalent products at lower prices, but they are not really offering the same things: the assurances of success, which can only be sold when there is a vast track record behind the company. Whenever an activity consists of producing a product or service whose future performance is both crucial to the buyer (think of the poor head of computer services, when the new system doesn't perform as promised!) and difficult to assess *ex ante*, either because the technology is new or complex, or because it is a service that, by definition, will only exist once it has been performed, then there is room for a profitable 'reputation effect'.

We have now given three reasons why a given activity may be performed by a company in a sustainable unique way (unique at least in the eyes of the buyer). If a design is patentable, if switching suppliers would entail a serious cost, if there is uncertainty *vis-à-vis* the performance of some suppliers, buyers will be prepared to pay more to go for a specific supplier, thus letting this particular company capture a large portion of the value being created. Conversely, if the buyer doesn't really care who is performing the activity, because it is performed equally well by all competitors (or so he thinks), then no particularly attractive profits can be made, for prices will reflect the strong competition that will ensue. Unless, of course, there are differentials in costs among the different suppliers, which is the second group of reasons why some activities are intrinsically profitable.

Consider, for instance, the group of activities necessary to produce the flat panel displays used in laptop computers. Although companies engaged in those activities don't disclose detailed data, there is some evidence that they are engaged in one of the most profitable activities in the whole system. There are very few suppliers, and practically all computer manufacturers, large or small, must buy from them. Why?

Manufacturing flat panel displays, with current technology, is an extremely difficult affair: tolerances are minimal, rejection rates extremely high. There are still many technical problems, ones that call for innovative solutions. Under these circumstances, only companies with a large market share can justify the huge investments in research and development required, and only companies with significant experience in manufacturing obtain acceptable costs. All this ensures that only a handful of companies can compete. Although many other companies could develop and manufacture the displays, their costs would be too high for them to make money, owing to lack of a large customer base over which to spread R&D costs and to the need to go down the *experience curve* that the current suppliers have already ridden.

The phenomenon by which larger producers obtain lower costs is called *economies of scale*. In most activities it does not apply: the difference in unit cost for a manufacturer of 100,000 keyboards or 1,000,000 keyboards is negligible. The same can be said of black and white computer screens or standard memory chips: beyond a certain size, all manufacturers obtain similar costs; and that size is not too large compared to the market, which makes it feasible for many competitors to coexist – and to compete their margins away.

But when economies of scale do apply, they are a source of profits, for the larger competitors have a built-in advantage. They can set prices at a level that will ensure good margins but at which potential competitors could not recover their investment.

Evidently economies of scale apply to activities, not to companies or products. Thus the minimum size for a computer manufacturer simply assembling purchased components is fairly small, for economies of scale in assembly are low. But the size necessary to compete successfully in flat panel displays is much larger, making this activity profitable. Whether the display is then sold to a computer assembler, or incorporated in a computer made by the display manufacturer itself is irrelevant: the value that goes with the economies of scale intrinsic to flat panel display manufacturing will accrue equally.

Economies of scale derive not only from R&D or manufacturing: volume purchases may obviously be a source of savings, as may advertising campaigns. In general, anything that has a large fixed cost (research, advertising, up-front investment) is more efficiently done if spread over as large a number of units as possible.

This fact determines the very important concept of minimum efficient size (MES): it is the minimum size at which a given activity must be performed in order to be as efficient as possible, from the point of view of economies of scale. In assembly or manufacturing activities it is determined by the underlying technology: to assemble a car by hand has a minimum efficient scale of one, for there are no cost advantages to size; but to assemble a car using the best current practices demands a volume of 200,000 to 300,000 every year. Any assembly runs below that figure would face a cost penalty.

Interestingly, the minimum efficient scale determines the

number of competitors that a given industry can sustain – this is the rationale for the bouts of concentration that industries go through every time there is a technological change. Thus every competitor in the automobile industry, given the huge development costs, now needs a volume of about 2,000,000 cars a year. Since the Western European market consists of about 13,000,000 units a year, it follows that no more than six manufacturers can survive over time. There might be less, but no more; if there were more, at least two of them would be operating below the minimum efficient scale, and therefore at a cost disadvantage. Lean times or increased imports would force them either out of business or to merge, which is exactly what is happening.

Of course the minimum efficient size is different for each activity, even within the same company. Consequently a company may find itself too large for some activities and too small for others. This is one of the main reasons why companies are opting to subcontract many activities they used to perform in-house, as we will see in Chapter 4. In any case a large minimum efficient size compared to the total size of the market determines that very few competitors can survive, making the activity intrinsically more profitable than an activity that can be performed equally well by hundreds of companies.

There are many other reasons why a company may obtain, when performing an activity, consistently lower costs than competitors, besides economies of scale. A labour-intensive activity may be performed in an area where labour costs are low, or the cost of the activity may be crucially dependent on a highly skilled labour force, or the company may enjoy a geographical location that lowers its costs, either by being close to its customers or to its supplies. Finally, some companies enjoy a cost advantage in some of their inputs, such as companies smelting aluminum in a country where electricity is cheap. In any case it is clear again that the cost advantage, and with it profits, applies to individual activities, not to the whole company performing the activities.

Whatever the reasons, if an activity is such that it cannot be performed equally well by all competitors, either because clients really prefer one competitor over another or because the costs are different, the foundations for substantial profits exist. In today's common parlance, it is said that those activities are protected by *barriers to entry* that preserve their profits. The important point is that these barriers are very different for the different activities that make up an industry and, for the same reason, for the different activities that make up a company.

If we go back to the map of the computer industry that I drew in Figure 2.1, we can analyse the intrinsic profitability of the different activities, by looking at the nature of the barriers to entry to that activity, and the key competitive factors necessary to succeed in them. But let me insist again: the final profitability depends on the profitability of the different activities. If a portable computer sells well because it has a unique battery system that ensures longer autonomy with less weight, it is to the manufacturer of the batteries that the profits will go, not to the assembler of the computer. Although what the buyer eventually buys is the result of a 'bundle' of activities, and although many of those activities may be provided by the same company, only some of them are really profitable, since they capture value through uniqueness or economies of scale. This was discussed, in the context of the computer industry, by an interesting article in the *Harvard Business Review*, 'The Computerless Computer Company'.[11] In essence, its point of view was that substantial value could only be captured in this business in activities that did not include manufacturing, and therefore the best computer company would be one that did not 'make computers'.

Without entering into the article's argument now (I will later challenge it), it follows from our discussion that the idea is not too far fetched. Consider the case of Apple Computer, a successful computer manufacturer. Apple owes its current success, basically, to the unique characteristics of the software that runs its Macintosh computers. Many people who have used one of them (this author included) are ready to pay (somewhat) more to enjoy its convenience. The manufacture of the computer itself, while being state of the art, hardly would generate profits on its own: there are perhaps hundreds of companies that could manufacture to the same standards of quality, and for similar costs, the same computer, provided they were authorized to use Apple's proprietary software designs, embodied in a few chips (not manufactured by Apple!). Apple, once it had designed the Macintosh operating system could conceivably have gone to IBM and offered the use of the system in IBM computers, and captured probably more profits than it has by heavily investing in assembly plants, which is not a very profitable activity, as we have seen. It would have captured more profits because, according to our argument, profits don't come from making computers, but from selling a superior basic software. If Apple had sold it through IBM, it would have sold no computers (where it does not make money anyway), but would have sold many more copies of its software (given IBM's bigger market share). By 'selling out', Apple, which is today's most profitable PC maker, would still be much more profitable.

If you find the argument far fetched, just look at Microsoft, for 'selling out' its basic software to IBM is exactly what Microsoft has done, and it has become, by far, the most successful 'computer' company of our days. On present trends Microsoft's market value will surpass IBM's somewhere in 1993. It is certainly larger than Apple's.

Interestingly, IBM could also have done that: produce a personal computer whose operating system (owned by IBM) and unique microprocessor (also owned by IBM) could be used by anybody else. This would have killed IBM's hardware business (as is about to happen anyway), but the most profitable computer companies in the world would not be Microsoft and Intel, but IBM! That of course would have required a completely different mentality and understanding of the industry from that developed at IBM over 40 extremely successful years of selling machines.

This kind of argument has led some people to generalize into saying that manufacturing is not a very interesting activity, and that Western companies should rather concentrate on the design of things, letting other people make them. I hope that the previous analysis has shown the shallowness of that argument. As long as an activity can be 'protected' by either inimitable qualities or sustainably lower costs, it will be profitable. As a matter of fact, most manufacturing activities are more defensible than most design activities: just think of the automobile industry, where technology is practically standard among manufacturers, and shape designs are simply subcontracted to design bureaux, which sell to anybody. The 'trick' is to manufacture better, and at a lower cost. Some companies do it, some others do not, and that year after year. Long after the laggards imitate the design and specifications of the successful companies, the quality and cost gap persists, and with it the good margins.

It is no surprise that manufacturing can be a very profitable activity. In fact, we have seen how, in the computer industry, it is in manufacturing some critical components such as flat panel displays that some of the best margins are being achieved. What cannot be very profitable, in the long term, is to assemble, *in a standard fashion*, components that can be bought in the open market, for *anybody* can do it. It is in that sense that manufacturing is less profitable than other activities – or not profitable at all. But there are many other kinds of manufacturing, from complex assembly (automobiles), to precision engineering (machine tools) and microtechnologies (electronic components), which have all the characteristics of profitable activities. Conversely, most service activities are very difficult to differentiate or perform at lower cost, so their profitability is mediocre at best.

At this point some of the reasons for the widely different success of companies competing in the computer industry should be clear. Certainly, besides the 'structural' reasons analysed so far, we cannot forget things as important as leadership, motivation, innovation, speed of implementation, etc. I shall come back to these in following chapters. But the basic way to frame the strategic territory of an industry, by decomposing it into its basic activities, and then analysing the profit potential of those activities, should be clear. I have used the computer industry extensively as the backdrop example to these ideas, but the activity-based analysis can evidently be applied to many other industries, from athletic apparel (as we saw Nike do) to automobiles (as we shall see in Chapter 4, the different arrangements along the business system determine profits all over), to banking (where experts maintain that there are at least five or six very different 'businesses' [we would call them activities] that can be dealt with jointly or separately).

Organizing the system

So far I've spent the chapter saying, in essence, that profitability is not a characteristic of industries, or even companies, but of activities. Why then the insistence in looking at the whole industry at the same time? The reason is that, if it is true that the profits companies operating in different activities make are a result of the profits made in each of the activities, there is another source of profits. The coordination of the different activities that end up producing the final product or service is also a costly, value-adding activity, and it can be performed in a more or less efficient (and defensible way), since the flow of goods along the industry system implies costs: in transportation, intermediate stocks, the need to adapt designs to different customers, the passage of information about pricing, technical character-istics, market evolution, etc.

Put another way, the total costs incurred in delivering a product or service to the final consumer (the value added) can be divided into two main categories: the activities necessary to manufacture or perform, and the costs incurred in putting those activities together. In essence, these are 'coordination activities', which glue together the design, manufacture and distribution activities that we have studied so far. These coordination activities may also be a source of profits, for they can be performed in a way that either makes the final product 'better' somehow in the eyes of the buyer, or enables companies to deliver it at a lower cost.

There are two classic ways to coordinate activities. The first consists of the old market mechanism. Thus a manufacturer of flat panel displays will decide to invest in colour units because there is a latent demand for them that will translate into high prices. Conversely, they may decide to stop investing in standard memory chips because there is a surplus of them, as evidenced by low prices.

For reasons that we shall examine in detail in the next chapter many companies find that to leave all coordination to market mechanisms is not desirable, and they decide therefore to coordinate by other means, i.e. by actually owning the units carrying out different activities. Thus the unit in charge of making flat panel displays inside IBM does so not because there was a direct demand for their units, but because some planner within the company decided that is what their portable computers needed. Specifications, volume, etc., are not subject to negotiation among independent profit-maximizing entities but to managerial coordination among less than fully autonomous units of a company. This second system is called 'vertical integration' – a company integrates several steps (activities) in a business system.

The next two chapters will analyse why and how these two different ways to coordinate activities may end up having very different results, *even if the activities themselves were performed in an identical fashion*. That is why companies, and the way they are organized, *do* matter. If we ignored these coordination costs, it would be irrelevant whether an activity was performed inside a company or outside, and the next two chapters will provide abundant examples of how that is certainly not the case. After that, Chapter 5 will go straight into the core of this book: that there is a better way to coordinate economic activities, one that yields better results by taking care more efficiently of the coordination activities and, in the end, by ensuring that the basic activities are carried out in the best possible way over time.

To be successful, a company must lower its costs: its own processing costs, the costs of its inputs, and the coordination costs. That's why the whole picture has to be taken into account, and it is a mistake to concentrate on just the company's costs. Coordination along the different steps is absolutely essential if one is to deal with uncertainties, inventories, information transfers, specialized assets, etc.

References

1 Something similar could be said of strategy's 'scientific' cousin, microeconomics, whose core doctrine is known as the 'theory of the firm'.

2 See, for instance, Andrews, Kenneth R., *The Concept of Corporate Strategy*, New York: Dow Jones-Irwin, 1971.

3 See Porter, Michael E., 'The contributions of industrial organization to strategic management', *Academy of Management Review*, vol. 6, no. 4, 1981.

4 'Let us adopt the working definition of an industry as the group of firms producing products that are close substitutes for each other.' Porter, Michael E., *Competitive Strategy*, New York: The Free Press, 1980, p. 5.

5 Interestingly, when Porter studies how some companies come to dominate industries worldwide, he does find it necessary to study whole industrial systems, acknowledging the crucial role played by suppliers and customers in one company's competitive excellence. Porter, Michael E., *The Competitive Advantage of Nations*, New York: The Free Press, 1990.

6 This is indeed well recognized by Michael Porter's second book, *Competitive Advantage*, although not all the implications are drawn. Porter, Michael E., *Competitive Advantage*, New York: The Free Press, 1985.

7 There is no little confusion about names. Many people, following M. Porter, use the term 'value chain', to refer to the series of activities performed by a company. Others call it 'value-added chain'. Yet those are looks at inside the company. I'm suggesting here taking a complete look at the creation of a product or service, from design and raw materials to after sales service (and recycling), regardless of how many companies perform those steps. In this sense the term 'business system' has been used by consulting companies, and has been refined conceptually by some academics, particuarly at IMD, in Lausanne. See, for instance, Xavier Gilbert and Paul Strebel, 'Developing Competitive Advantage', in H. Mintzberg (ed.), *The*

Strategy Process, Englewood Cliffs, New Jersey: Prentice-Hall, 1987.

8 There have been makers of IBM mainframe-compatible machines, but they have always had to pay a big penalty in terms of costs, for they had to wait for IBM to introduce models, with huge technical difficulty, to reverse-engineer them. For this reason, they never constituted a real threat to IBM.

9 One American company, called Paperback Software, did the equivalent to a PC clone: it started selling a spreadsheet that took the same commands as Lotus 1-2-3, although the program was written in a different way. Fortunately for Lotus, the American legal system prevented the company from making many inroads.

10 See 'Tetra-Pak', by Ralf Boscheck, IMD case, 1992.

11 Andrew S. Rappaport and Halevi Shmuel, 'The Computerless Computer Company', *Harvard Business Review*, July–August, 1991.

Part Two   The Three Ways to Organize a Business System

3 The old system: organization through vertical integration

'That component is too critical for us to out-source it. We simply must do it ourselves.' This very common statement describes what vertical integration is all about: the ownership, within the same company, of separate activities within the business system. For example, a paper manufacturer becomes 'integrated' when it buys a timber farm to obtain its basic raw material direct. Another example could be IBM, which, as we saw, manufactures many of the components that go into its computers, which it assembles and distributes through different channels.

Every company is, at least, partially integrated, because a completely de-integrated company would consist of one person working behind a (rented) desk, with a telephone, acting as a middleman between sellers and buyers. Some businesses are like this, e.g. estate agents renting out flats and houses, but they are few and far between.

On the other hand, no company is totally integrated. There have been some extreme cases of organizations such as Kodak, which even had its own livestock, from which it got the gelatin it needed to manufacture photographic products, and its own woodlands, so that it could manufacture the paper needed for Kodak prints. But even in these extreme cases there are always some products the company continues to buy from outside suppliers as part of its operations. And then, things have to be sold. Kodak never owned the distributors and shops that took its products to the final customer. If we go back to the terminology introduced in Chapter 2, we can say that a completely de-integrated company would only carry out *one* activity of the business system, while a fully integrated one would be involved in *all* activities. The first case is relatively uncommon, the second practically nonexistent. To finish the definition mode, when a company starts performing an activity traditionally carried out by its suppliers, it is said that it integrates 'backwards'. When the company moves to performing activities closer to the final consumer (thus substituting for its immediate customers), it integrates 'forward'.

In this chapter we shall analyse the main reasons why companies engage in vertical integration, examine the soundness of those reasons, and study the problems that vertical integration almost necessarily implies. In the end the aim is to come to a clear conclusion on when and why it may be better to coordinate two or more activities of the business system by owning them instead of leaving that coordination to market mechanisms. As we know, this will only be the case if vertical integration either lowers the cost of performing some of the activities or the cost of coordinating them.

Why do companies integrate?

In real life, companies make the decision to carry out on their own other activities of the business system for a number of reasons. One, seen in the example of Ford's, is that the company may not find a supplier (or reseller) with enough quality or volume to meet the company's requirements. Another may simply be a desire to grow: unable to sell more amounts of its product, the company decides to 'add more value', i.e. to be responsible for more of the activities that make up the product. By doing this, the company becomes 'bigger' in terms of employees, capital invested, etc., even if units sold remain the same: it is a way to grow without having to beat competitors, for all you have to do is 'fire' your suppliers. Yet another reason may be the desire to keep a technology secret, by not sharing it with any supplier or customer in activities that, for their proximity, might expose it.

In any case what matters to us is not why companies integrate, but in what cases integration makes sense. In the terminology of Chapter 2 this is akin to asking in what cases the carrying out of different activities by the same company can result in a *better* coordination among them, either by lowering the cost, or by making the final product somehow more attractive, by reducing its coordination costs. From Chapter 2 we know that this is the only way a company can expect to increase its profits.

A weak argument

Let us start, to clear the way, with a very widespread misunderstanding: many people see vertical integration as a way to increase their profits, by simply capturing the margins that the players in those activities were making. In reasoning so, companies often make serious conceptual (and, eventually, practical) errors. Let us see why.

Companies often have to decide between buying a component (or service) and manufacturing it themselves. In these cases it is usual to calculate what the internal manufacturing costs would be (raw materials, new machinery, possible employment of new workers) and compare them with the price quoted by suppliers. When doing that calculation, it very often seems to be more economical to manufacture in-house, for one simple reason: while the price set by suppliers includes everything, not only direct costs but also its profits, the company usually only includes direct costs in its calculations. This is a serious mistake, because general operating costs (and profits!) come into all the company's activities, although in the short term this may not seem to be true. It is rare, for example, that the time management spends on starting up production of the new component is calcu-lated, though it is in fact a significant cost, if only because of the time that can no longer be dedicated to the usual business of the company.

In the same way it is not usual to expect a return on the capital invested in producing the component (machinery, stocks of raw materials and intermediate products, etc.) to at least match the company's normal return. When all these costs are added up, you normally find that the price offered by suppliers is not so bad after all. In fact, later on, we shall see that there are good reasons for thinking that in principle, the price offered by suppliers is lower than the actual total costs for the company starting production – although it may not always seem that way at first sight.

Vertical integration is frequently seen as a means of taking over the margin made by those either supplying or marketing the product in question, or even more important, the famous 'middlemen'. It is often heard, for example, 'I sell to the distributor at £100, and he sells to the end-customer at £130. If I sell direct to the customer, cutting out the distributor, I can sell at £110, and be much more competitive as I am selling the product more cheaply and on top of that make more money.' This reasoning is not only relatively common but also extremely erroneous and dangerous. Here is an example to illustrate the point.

Let us take the case of a company that manufactures textiles for the clothing industry. These textiles are normally sold through outside retailers. To simplify matters, let's say that the factory sells direct to the retailers and that the different prices set and margins made throughout the whole chain of manufacturing and marketing processes are those detailed in Table 3.1.

It seems that 'there is a lot of money to be made' between the manufacturer and the end-user, and that the manu-

Table 3.1

	Purchase Price (£)	Costs	Margin	Sale Price (£)
Manufacturer	10	10	15	35
Retailer	35	15	20	70

facturer could quite easily open up his own retail outlets and through them sell direct to the public. If so, for each metre of material produced he would still make his £15, but also the £20 margin made by the retailer, making a total profit of £35 each time. Or better still, he could give up part of the already inflated margin (more than double the original margin) and sell to the public at only £65. By doing this, besides earning £30 per metre of material sold, he might attract more customers by selling cheaply, which would mean that he could manufacture more and maybe increase profits there too. The logic behind this exercise seems flawless. Money is made at the factory stage, because sales are good, and money is made at the retail stage too. The middleman has been profitably cut.

The flaw in this argument lies in only demanding profitability from one activity in the system, which tends to be the 'core activity', i.e. the activity that the company has traditionally performed. But money has to be made everywhere. What happens to the profitability of the shop if the sale price is lowered from £70 to £65 per metre? One thing is clear, it will drop noticeably because it means the retail profit margin shrinks from £20 to £15/metre, which is a drop of 25 per cent.

The fact that the shop may have a high margin does not necessarily mean that its profitability is also high. Profitability is not only based on gross margins but also on the investment made. For the manufacturer in our example to achieve the margins mentioned, he will have to invest a certain amount in starting up from scratch, or buying, a chain of shops. If part of the normal margin made by the shops is passed on to the customer through a reduction in the sale price, the investment made in the shops will not be very profitable, and the profitability of the company will drop as a result. If prices are kept at the original level, then the profitability of the retail outlets will also remain the same, but then the hoped-for 'advantages' of vertical integration will not materialize. What will actually be happening is that the company will be moving into a new activity – retailing – which may or may not be profitable from a structural point of view. If it is not profitable, then it is not worth moving into. If it is, you can be sure that there will be high barriers to entry protecting it.

False logic like this is often used by those shopkeepers who sell at very low prices and justify them with the explanation that 'we are also the manufacturers'. According to this reasoning, they can sell at a cheaper price because they manufacture the goods themselves, so their costs are lower than if they have to buy from an outside manufacturer, who would be selling at a mark-up. Obviously this argument in itself does not make any sense, because they are either going to lose money at the manufacturing stage or at the retail stage. You cannot expect to run two businesses profitably with just one margin.

In any case it is very important to understand one particular point: that simply by controlling two links in the chain of production and marketing processes you can actually set arbitrary prices for sales between them, but that this in itself can never be a way of making money. It is impossible to make (or lose) money from selling things to yourself. The supposed savings at one end would turn into costs (lack of profit) at the other end. Let's go back to our textile company. There are certain occasions when integration may be justified as a means of survival for the business. If the textile company is having problems selling its products, it could think about setting up its own shops to guarantee an outlet for them, and so avoid the factory facing bankruptcy. Once again, this argument is a false and dangerous one.

In the first place, if by acquiring the shops the company has to lower margins as we described before, then the company – already in difficulties on the manufacturing front – is attempting to solve these difficulties by moving into another area where margins are also low. Not a good idea! What is more, to set up a chain of shops would really only be a way of jumping from the frying pan into the fire without tackling the real problem, which is the poor sales figures at the factory. Furthermore, if these poor sales figures merely reflect low-quality merchandise or old-fashioned designs, then the shops will not be able to sell the merchandise anyway, with the net result that the company will lose money on both fronts –

manufacturing and retailing. If the problem is one of costs, because the company cannot produce goods competitively, the only thing it will do will be to transfer the problem to the shops which will have to buy a raw material (textiles) which is not competitively priced. What is more, not only are the problems left unsolved, but they are actually made worse, because top management will probably have to engage in the problems created by entering a new business, thus leaving the core business unattended. In general, jumping from the frying pan into the fire is not a sensible strategy for a company. It is understandable that a company might want to 'buy up' its customers in order to guarantee sales, but it is clear that all this does is pass on the problem down the line with the consequent effects.

We can certainly generalize from this simplified example, following the reasoning of Chapter 2: it is less than clear that, for being engaged in two different activities of the business system, the company will be more profitable. This extra profitability will only accrue if, without negatively affecting the profitability of one activity, the fact that company engages in it somehow improves its profitability in another, or reduces the coordination costs. It is impossible to improve margins by simply selling to oneself.

Other arguments for vertical integration

Why could that be? Let's take a look at three cases, which may either be based on technological or strategic reasons. Let's start by looking at those cases where technological considerations are all-important,

When vertical integration saves costs for technological reasons

Imagine a steel manufacturing company that, among other things, smelts iron ore to produce steel, and then hot-rolls the steel. Steel is produced from iron ore in a blast furnace, a technical process that is totally separate from rolling, which actually takes place in a rolling mill. In principle there is no reason why a steel manufacturing firm should not concentrate its activities on producing steel in ingots, for example, which it could then sell to another company to roll. This second company, however, would have to heat the ingot again before rolling it, using up a great deal of energy. An integrated company, which could roll the ingot the minute it came out the blast furnace – when it was still hot - would save on energy costs and be more competitive as a result. Note that in this case there would be a total saving. Unlike the previous examples, we are not talking now about 'saving' a margin, only to lose it again on another front, but about a real difference in the total cost of the hot-rolled steel.

This example, which is the classic one put forward in economics textbooks, is a good illustration of how there may be technical advantages – closely linked to the production or marketing of the product – which support vertical integration. Generally speaking, whenever two stages in the production or marketing processes of a product are undertaken consecutively and the total costs of these are reduced, it will be the more integrated company that will be the most competitive. But, let's just make this point again. The way to find out if a saving on costs is actually made is to analyse if, simply by being performed by the same company, one of the costly stages in the total production process can be eliminated. If the saving is really only made because the company can now sell goods to itself at a cheaper price than an outside supplier, without any real streamlining of the process itself, then once again we are dealing with a false saving as described in detail earlier.

Savings can also be made when the company can apply its expertise to a new area of business. Take for example, purchasing. If a company has a good, established purchasing department and, because of the high volume of purchases, manages to get its supplies at a particularly good price, then it may make sense for it to manufacture the intermediate products, using a cheaper raw material than its suppliers of intermediate products. In this case the company would be more efficient than its suppliers (of intermediate products) since it could buy the original raw materials (or any other input) cheaper than they could, because of the high volume of purchases made.

A similar point can be made about the general functions of the company. If it has very good management, or a personnel recruitment and development policy that guarantees particularly high-quality staff, it may be able to manufacture its own supplies (or move on to market its own products) more efficiently than a less sophisticated outside supplier (or customer). In the end this may be the reason why many of the largest companies integrated their operations decades ago: finding outside suppliers with the sufficient level of managerial sophistication was far from easy, and companies found it more efficient to simply do things 'their way'.

All these are reasons that explain why vertical integration may be the best way to lower *total* costs. But vertical integration may also be appropriate for strategic reasons, ones that have to do more with the preservation or acquisition of new competitive advantages, or with coordination costs.

Vertical integration to defend or obtain competitive advantages in specific activities

A company may find itself in a position where it must become integrated in a different part of the process from its own core activities simply in order to preserve these activities. Let us take a company with a high level of technology.

Sometimes the supplies needed by this company are so specialized that, together with the general specifications of the product, it would have to give its suppliers so much confidential information that they could use it to become direct competitors or pass on the information to an existing competitor. Something of the same sort can be said about marketing (selling), which may require such detailed knowledge of the product to be sold that the company may not want to give the task to anyone outside. Therefore the company must become integrated in order to protect its key competitive advantage and prevent it from being squandered or taken over by an outside agent.

It is also possible for vertical integration to be used as a strategy of attack. The aim here is not to defend any competitive advantages, but to obtain them, partly thanks to integration. This happens, for example, in the case of a company that, by becoming integrated, increases the volume of production of some subcomponent it was using in the manufacture of other products or in other processes and so achieves economies of scale in other areas of its operations.

It is also quite usual for a company to opt for vertical integration as the best policy when its general strategy is to underline the high quality of its products compared to others on the market, and so it believes that it is the only company that can manufacture components of sufficient quality for its requirements, or when it only wants to sell through its own shops, as it sees this as the only way to maintain the quality and image of the product. If this is true, then it is clear that a strategy of vertical integration, if it is carried out well, can turn a business into an unassailable competitor.

Vertical integration can be used as a learning device. Sometimes it is crucial for a company to understand underlying technologies in some of the components it uses, for changes in those may actually affect the competitiveness of the activities it is involved with. In addition, integrating forward may be a way to understand the rest of its clients better: it makes sense for McDonald's to own a number of its restaurants, so it understands the business better, thus increasing its competitiveness.

Vertical integration to lower coordination costs

Vertical integration can also 'save' the company money when the relation between company and supplier is particularly costly, either because the information that must be passed on to the supplier is substantial or continuous, or may change. In these cases there would be an 'economy in the transaction' that could be quite a significant saving. If working with a supplier implies constant changes in specifications, joint learning, contacts at multiple levels, etc., some companies may find that it is more efficient to own the supplier outright.

In any case we could generalize by saying that vertical integration is justified when leaving the coordination of two activities to the market (i.e. maintaining a policy of concentrating on only a few activities, buying the inputs and selling the outputs to outsiders), either raises the cost of one of the activities, or weakens the company's ability to differentiate it in the eyes of the next customer.

All the previous arguments, both right and wrong, have led many companies over the years to integrate. In a way the discussion over vertical integration is a bit like the discussion over diversification. Whatever is said about it, one thing is clear: practically all large companies do it.

This extension of the practice does not mean, however, that it is free of disadvantages. Again as in the case of diversification, a strong current of opinion has evolved in the last few years against it. In the remainder of this chapter we shall see why.

Disadvantages of vertical integration

The parallel with diversification is a particularly apt one, for engaging in vertical integration is, in essence, engaging in diversification. As we discussed at length in Chapter 2, each activity of the business system is in fact a different business, in the sense that the technology, optimum size, distribution methods, etc. may be different.

At this point a serious question arises. If vertical integration consists, essentially, of entering a new business, it must face the barriers to entry to that business; for, as we saw in the previous chapter, any activity that is profitable must be somehow protected from competition, or it would not be profitable. Thus if the new activity a company wants to engage in is profitable, it follows that it is difficult to enter. If, conversely, entry is easy . . . where will the profits be and why bother?

Evidently the answer traditionally given tends to fall into some of the arguments discussed above, most of the time into the weaker ones, such as 'we know the market', 'we have a captive client', etc. All this does not solve the basic problem: if carrying out the new activity has any profits in it, it will be because doing it efficiently is somehow difficult, either because of the technology is complex, or the necessary volume is very large, or any of the reasons put forward in Chapter 2.

Together with barriers to entry, diversification often has to contend with problems specific to the company itself and this is also the case of vertical integration. We have already emphasized that integration can mean a company moving into an area of business completely different from its previous activities. Remaining in the same industry may disguise huge technological, production, and competitive differences between the businesses, which may require different skills and expertise to those that the company employed so successfully before. Inexperienced management may lead to serious mistakes being made or, at the very least, to the company being much less efficient than a supplier specializing in the activity and with many years of experience already in the bag.

Both these reasons – the company's inexperience in a new area and the economies of scale enjoyed by the supplier, who is not just producing for himself – explain why, in general, suppliers' prices are in fact lower than the costs for a company that becomes integrated. The latter is in fact, when it comes to purchasing, competing against a supplier manufacturing a greater volume (economies of scale) and with much more experience. In these circumstances it is an almost sure thing that the outside supplier will be more competitive, i.e. it will actually be cheaper for the company to buy from outside than to manufacture the product itself. Only if the supplier had a ridiculously high mark-up on its products would it be worthwhile for the company to manufacture for itself, even if it meant that its costs were higher than those of its supplier. But, just remember again, if the supplier is able to mark up high profit margins on the product, it is because its business is protected by high barriers to entry, and so it will not be easy for the company to break into this area of business.

Lack of experience in this new business will probably put great demands on management's time and attention, which can lead to neglecting the running of the company's core activities. That is one cost of integration that must be taken into account and one generally ignored. It is not just that the management has to devote time to the new area of business but also that at least some of the limited resources of the company are also diverted to that area, such as the money needed to install new manufacturing equipment which could perhaps be put to better use improving the competitive position of the company in the area of production it was already engaged in.

In spite of all these problems, we have already seen how most large companies end up integrating their operations. The reason is that those companies have all grown up on the exploitation of some outstanding competitive advantage, normally gained in one or just a few activities. Those activities turn out to be so profitable that the company can afford to indulge in many others of doubtful profitability.

The problems created by such behaviour do not show overnight, however. Thus vertical integration may pose problems that only appear in the long term. We have seen so far generic reasons why vertical integration may not be a good idea to start with. But perhaps more important is what we could call the *dynamic problems*, i.e. the reasons why vertical integration may, slowly but surely, cause a deterioration of company's performance. We shall do that by analysing how it affects the three key strategic characteristics of a company, namely, its efficiency, its flexibility, and its capacity to innovate.

When vertical integration zaps efficiency

The first way to lose efficiency through vertical integration is by performing the new activities with less efficiency than the former subcontractors. As we have seen, this is most likely.

Let us think first about the barriers to entry that protect every profitable activity. In reality the new area of activity being developed by the company was already being undertaken by other companies (including the original supplier). The competitive situation in that particular activity may mean that these companies earn a lot of money or not according to the structural analysis in Chapter 2. If it is not a very profitable activity, it would seem, in principle, a better idea to carry on buying from suppliers, because prices are already low and there is no real reason for moving into a business with a low profit margin.

If, on the other hand, the suppliers are earning a lot of money, it must be because there are high barriers to entry protecting their market, for otherwise the force of competition would have already pushed margins down. In these circumstances any company considering vertical integration must also consider the costs incurred by scaling these barriers to entry and becoming a real competitor to its previous suppliers.

Possibly the most significant barrier to entry is that of economies of scale. When a company seriously considers manufacturing a component, it must decide on what the minimum production must be for it to be absolutely cost-effective. If the company's own requirements are lower than this minimum level of production and yet it still wishes to go ahead with integration, it will find itself left with two alternatives: either (a) manufacture only its own requirements, operating less efficiently than its suppliers (who can benefit from economies of scale) and, by extension, less efficiently than its competitors, who buy from those other suppliers, or (b) manufacture more than its own requirements in order to gain from economies of scale, and sell the surplus production on the open market.

This second option brings with it significant problems. Besides the fact that a sales network, no matter how small, must be set up, it may also mean selling to your own direct competitors unless the component can be used in a completely different industry. Maintaining supplier–client relations with direct competitors, although not impossible, usually tends to be difficult both in the short and particularly in the long term.

Another reason why efficiency may suffer, in the longer term, is that, within many vertically integrated companies, one finds a lot of 'internal monopolies'. Certainly the company competes in the open market with its final products, but whole divisions that are insulated from market pressures may exist within it, since they sell most of their production to a captive customer. This, which at the beginning may be even a good idea, for it saves on marketing costs, easily degenerates into all the inefficiencies associated with monopolies and central planning. In effect, as we saw in Chapter 1, vertically integrating a whole system is something akin to the centrally planned economies of former Eastern Europe, with all their possible advantages (no marketing 'waste', no 'excessive' competition, ability to plan long term . . .) and all their real disadvantages (planning mistakes, magnified by lack of alternative, lack of incentive, innovation as the ultimate disturbance . . .).

The managers in charge of these internal monopolies end up developing a mentality akin to that of the managers of *any* monopoly, where efficiency and service are not the key goals, but rather the attainment, at any cost, of clearly set long-term production plans; and, more generally, the preservation of the *status quo*. As we will see later, some organizational devices can be set up to try to lessen those problems, but they never really go away: no matter how seriously a company instructs its divisions to 'compete with external suppliers', in a situation of low demand and high fixed costs orders go almost always to the internal supplier, and everybody knows that.

As we have seen, many companies start integrating, for whatever reason, when they are engaged in a very profitable activity of the business system. It is the profits earned in the profitable activity that in fact provide the company with the funds necessary to get into other activities. One of the worst problems is that the fat margins allowed by a well-protected activity tend, logically, to generate fat costs. Thus companies that are very successful tend to offer better employment terms to their employees, have nicer facilities, etc. That is probably appropriate, for there are good margins to go around. The company may also indulge in excessive bureaucracy and what is generally described as 'fat', for the profits are there to sustain it, and the barriers to entry to protect them.

The problem is that, if the company goes into activities that are not so intrinsically profitable, it will probably carry its 'fat business' mentality with it. It is indeed very difficult to have a company where different parts (activities) offer very different employment and business conditions. To follow our example of Chapter 2, it is quite clear that people engaged in designing operating systems for IBM mainframes will, sooner or later, reach above-average salaries, for they are producing above-average results. But, after a number of years of successful operations, all IBM employees will tend to enjoy above-average conditions, when they are not generating above-average margins, for most are engaged in not particularly profitable activities.

This has a terrible implication: the profitability of the not-very-profitable activities of an integrated company will normally be below average, for their costs will be above average, because of the 'spill over' effect from the truly profitable activities. That ensures a 'built-in' handicap for the integrated company: instead of reinvesting the funds generated by the truly profitable activities in those activities, to ensure their continued success, they are diverted to non-profitable business. When, for any reason, the above-average profits of the 'core activities' decline, the whole company unravels fast.

Vertically integrated companies tend to impose not only the costs of the most successful activities on to the others, but also the 'organizational culture' characteristic of the successful activities. This 'mismatch' of cultures is yet one more source of inefficiency in many integrated companies.

This built-in inefficiency, which is observed in many companies that suddenly discover that they can get inputs outside at a lower cost, is compounded by the 'bureaucratic mentality' that develops because there is no real contact with clients who can easily choose a different supplier. The bureaucratic mentality is further enshrined by the need to coordinate many different activities of the business, at least some of which will not be very profitable in themselves, as we have seen. Thus a whole layer of managers develops, ones whose mission is to 'protect' the current situation, where the company can make profits thanks to its advantages in a few activities. That situation may last for a time but, when the root of the advantages disappears, the company finds itself with three problems: a competitive core, which is no more; a large number of activities with marginal or negative profitability; and a large bureaucracy trained to make sure nothing changes.

This sorry situation is exactly the state of many of the large integrated companies as soon as the core of its profitability deteriorates, as we saw. What seems to be their main strength (the fact that they 'controlled' the whole business system) quickly turns out to be their main liability: a huge bureaucratic system engaged in organizing not very profitable activities, with a serious lack of understanding of the real costs (and therefore profitability) of the different parts of the system. As mentioned, IBM and GM could be examples of that, but so could many large banks, or even apparently profitable companies such as Philips, Siemens or some large Japanese manufacturers.

Loss of flexibility

As well as having many of the inherent problems of diversification, vertical integration also lacks some of its advantages. Indeed integration concentrates risks in the same industry. By increasing its fixed costs significantly, the company puts itself in a much riskier position if there is a possible drop in sales caused by the general weakness of the industry, or for any other reason. If difficult times arrive, then a company with only variable costs will find itself in a much better position because if, for whatever reason, sales should slump, the company only needs to stop buying from its suppliers to compensate. If the company is integrated, it will have a lot more money invested in fixed assets and staff that cannot be fully exploited.

Indeed integration can take flexibility away from a company by forcing it to be tied to a specific technology. If the company buys from a supplier and a new technological change is introduced in the component, the only thing the company has to do is to go to a new supplier to keep on top. If, on the other hand, the company is integrated, then it will find itself forced to dismantle equipment that is now obsolete or to use a component that technologically is no longer competitive. Integration therefore may increase the technological risks for the company and delay its market responsiveness. Thus General Motors was very late in introducing electronic fuel injection when it had the technology at its disposal, because it had invested in a large carburettor plant, which would be rendered obsolete by the technological advance.

For that reason vertical integration is typical in developed markets, where the technology is not likely to change much, where the companies cannot grow much more by increasing sales and, as a result, have substantial resources to invest. So the trend is to increase, if not the sales, the added value of the company through vertical integration. The risk is that of unforeseen circumstances causing either the technological or competitive rules of the game to change or the industry to enter a period of change or uncertainty. If this happens, the integrated companies are those worst placed to compete.

This was the case for General Motors. For years it was the undisputed market leader, with a 50 per cent market share. General Motors enjoyed such economies of scale compared to its two main competitors, Ford and Chrysler, that this made it the lowest cost producer, and since the company was not interested in increasing its market share for fear of an anti-monopoly probe, this leadership in costs was translated into consistently higher margins than those of its competitors. Its huge sales volume also meant that its degree of integration was far greater than that of Ford or Chrysler since, even though it was only manufacturing for itself, its divisions produced as much as Ford and Chrysler's suppliers. But when the stability of the market was altered by the introduction of new and aggressive competitors (firstly the Japanese with their small cars and the European companies with their luxury models) who brought with them overwhelming technological innovations and cost advantages, General Motors found its hands were tied far tighter than Ford, which could react by demanding more flexibility from its suppliers or by getting supplies from Japan or Europe, whereas General Motors had to work around the problem of its own non-competitive divisions. The outcome of a number of years of uncertainty, restructuring, plant closures etc., is that General Motors is now the car manufacturer with the highest costs, its market share has fallen to nearly 30 per cent and its profits have essentially disappeared.

Flexibility may also be lost in the marketing side. Consider a typical case. A large company buys one of its traditional suppliers, in order to integrate vertically. The supplier, now part of the company, may have had as customers some of the company's competitors, which, if they can help it, will no longer want to buy from that supplier, with the result that the investment made in such an acquisition loses some of its profitability. This is what happened to Mercedes Benz when it acquired AEG. BMW immediately stopped considering AEG as a reliable supplier, as it had become just another division of its main rival. Obviously AEG's profitability suffered as a result. In general, the result is catastrophic if, by losing those clients, sales volume drops below minimum efficient size.

Thus vertical integration, in the cases when a company must sell part of its internal production in the market, can lead to paralysing conflicts of interest. Sharp has tried to tout its video cameras by fitting them with a colour visor, which the other manufacturers cannot make economically. But Sharp has no particular competitive advantages in making the cameras. By trying to make money where it can't, it could jeopardize its strong leadership in the activity where it can make money, i.e. the colour displays. If not selling the displays to other manufacturers implies keeping production levels relatively low, Sharp may be inadvertently zapping its competitiveness, and may also be strongly encouraging other competitors to enter that business. A policy of aggressively selling to everybody would probably ensure their leadership in displays (a very profitable activity), but hurt their sales of cameras (perhaps not such a profitable activity for them after all). This idea of 'forcing' clients to 'buy' something mediocre from the company if they want to obtain that which is really good is very common, and seen as a way to 'pad' profits. But all it does is misallocate margins: if customers really want the unique part, let them pay for it, and obtain the rest wherever they want.

One last point remains: the loss of control resulting from integration. Like many of the points already studied this is paradoxical since one of the 'qualitative' reasons usually put forward in favour of integration is that 'by producing the component ourselves, we guarantee better control over supply because we do not have to depend on an outside supplier'. Once again this argument is in many cases a false one.

In fact it is often easier to control an outside supplier than an internal division. One can always threaten a supplier with replacement, a threat that does not work so well against an internal division. What can you do if the internal division turns out a product of irregular quality? One can easily replace a supplier unless there is some particular reason, such as one of those listed at the beginning. Why should an internal division manufacture a better quality product or deliver more punctually? It is not reasonable to believe that, simply by integrating, problems are going to disappear. In fact they will probably get worse given the lack of experience of the company in manufacturing the component.

So, in conclusion, if a reliable supplier lets you down in a competitive, open situation, it is because he makes a mistake. It is not realistic to think that your company will never make them. Only if the supplier enjoys a quasi-monopolistic position could we consider that an internal division could be more easily controlled and vertical integration justified. But, let's emphasize this point again, if that quasi-monopoly is stable, it will be because of the extremely high barriers to entry to the market, and the company will have to pay dearly to break through them.

Generally speaking, an internal corporate division has less reason to produce well than an external supplier, who can be easily motivated simply by placing orders with him or not. In the case of internal transactions, complex systems of transfer prices and control mechanisms have to be set up, and, no matter how hard you try, you can never really reproduce the same flexibility and motivation as found on the open market. It is often simpler and more profitable to look out for alternative suppliers to those already used by the company if it considers the existing ones are too powerful, perhaps because they can take advantage of the little competition in their industry. To give some of the orders to a company experienced in related areas and wanting to diversify into the production of the product in question, or coming from a country where it already has experience, is a much simpler way of improving control over your suppliers than taking the step of vertical integration.

When vertical integration is a barrier to learning

For all these reasons, it is not uncommon that coordinating the different activities through their common ownership ends up being less efficient than coordinating them through the market. But vertical integration may also have an insidious, long-term effect: it may hinder a company's ability to learn, which is its only assurance of continued success.

It is well established that the main sources of innovation are a company's customers and suppliers.[1] By integrating vertically, one ensures that many of the activities of the business system don't have direct access to them. Although at the time of the integration the technology used may be start of the art, it is a matter of time before, devoid of the main creative stimulus, the part of the company that performs the isolated activity will fall behind.

This is compounded by the not-invented-here syndrome, which easily creeps into integrated companies. When the corporate incentives go to 'doing things our way', it is extremely easy to try to reinvent the wheel at every turn, at a great cost in terms of efficiency. Again, companies that enjoy a very robust source of profits (*de jure* or *de facto* monopolies or oligopolies in some activities) can indulge in that behaviour, but they carry a huge liability for the day things change, as they always end up doing.

Guidelines for decision-making on vertical integration

To summarize our previous discussion: vertical integration makes sense if and only if it lowers the costs in some of the activities, somehow improves the company's performance in them, or affords better coordination than what could be achieved in an open market. In all other circumstances it is not only not helpful, it is positively harmful.

In this context, how do you make a decision on vertical integration? Although obviously every case is different, a few questions can give orientation.

What are the real advantages being sought?

First we must expect any possible vertical integration to bring with it one or some of the benefits or advantages detailed before, whether they are real savings in costs or competitive gains. If this is not clear, it is better not to do it. Reducing costs only through selling to oneself more cheaply than before, as we have seen, is not enough. But even when we are sure that the decision to go ahead with vertical integration would bring with it certain advantages, then we must be sure that the negative points do not outweigh the benefits. In any case it will still be necessary to take steps to reduce as far as possible the impact of these negative points. Let us see how this can be done.

We should study whether integration would reduce costs on the technological front, as in the case of the steel ingots, which would not have to be reheated before hot rolling. Or in the case of a newspaper, if an in-house printing department means that the text can be laid out automatically (the journalist punches the text direct on to the machine, which puts it together and then prints) and so allows more flexibility if there are any last minute changes, which may improve the paper's quality, then it may make sense to spend the money and effort on installing and maintaining the printing machinery.

What are the main costs of vertical integration, and how can they be lowered?

The same can be said about integration for strategic reasons. If integration is the only reasonable way of protecting the core operations of the company or the only way to gain vital know-how, then it is a good idea. But, as with any strategic decision, it is very important to reduce as far as possible the costs. It is, in fact, very common to think that, because it is a strategic decision and since it is not necessary to justify it in relation to short-term costs, then these costs do not have to be justified at all. This is a mistake that usually turns out to be an expensive one. If it seems important to become integrated for strategic reasons you have to take into account the real cost of the process (in those terms already discussed: low efficiency, diversion of resources, etc.) and compare them with the hoped-for benefits.

One method of integration offering nearly all the advantages of integration and reducing the effect of many of its disadvantages is called 'tapered integration'. This means that a company becomes integrated for only part of its requirements of any one component, and buys the rest from outside suppliers. In this way the advantages are the acquisition of new technology and firm control over suppliers, which is maintained by the threat of stopping the flow of orders and manufacturing own supplies, much more convincing now since the company is already doing so to a certain extent. Yet the flexibility of receiving some supplies from outside, at variable costs, taking advantage at the same time of the experience, technological know-how and volume of specialized suppliers, is not lost. In this sense it is very different to say that a company is 50 per cent integrated, meaning than it manufactures all of component A and buys all of component B, to when it is 50 per cent integrated because it manufactures half of A and half of B. This second option may be the safer one from a competitive point of view. It obviously depends on whether the volume of production of the component is high with respect to possible economies of scale, or this option would increase the costs too much.

But, in spite of all these possibilities, vertical integration is becoming more and more the strategy of the past. In the next section, we will analyse how the precarious balance between advantages and disadvantages is being lost in favour of de-integration.

Why the problems are outweighing the advantages more and more

There are four sets of trends that strongly push for de-integration: social, motivational, economic and technological. These are undoubtedly related, and reinforce each other.

Social trends have made working for a large (generally meaning integrated) company far less important. The old sense of security is gone, and two-income families can afford to be somewhat more venturesome. At the same time our culture has led people to demand more personal satisfaction from their jobs, asking for decision-making power and participative management. All this works in the direction of making small, focused units more attractive to gifted individuals than large bureaucracies. In as much as we move towards knowledge-intensive industries, it is precisely the capacity to attract and motivate those individuals that will determine long-term competitive advantage, which reduces the attractiveness of vertical integration.

But there are a number of 'harder' economic trends that favour de-integration. First of all, the emergence of a market for corporate governance makes it more difficult for large companies to get away with inefficient, empire-building integration. In effect the buy-out activity typical of the 1980s allows a 'raider' to take a company, strip it of its non-profitable bits, and sell it when it is more competitive, by concentrating on its core activities. This used to be impossible in the past, but right now only the very largest companies are exempt from the threat, and then only for so long. In spite of the current 'pause to breathe', this process of 'restructuring' will go on, for, contrary to conventional wisdom, it does add value – taking apart companies which are inefficiently integrated is a good way to liberate economic potential.

The process is spreading. As economic difficulties grow, and international competition becomes keener, the phenomenon of dis-integration, adjusted for the different kind of capitalism practised there, is coming to continental Europe and Japan, where many of the large groups are taking a hard look at their engagement in too many steps of the business system.

But also the very advancement of the different economies is fostering de-integration. We saw how the lack of qualified subcontractors has led companies in the past to integrate. As a market for such services develops, the rationale disappears . . . and the disadvantages start to weigh. Thus, much of the statistically recorded growth in services at the expense of manufacturing in the last decades is due not to a real change in activity but to a change in integration. When a large industrial company has an in-house travel department, that department's employees and output show up as 'manufacturing'. When the company dissolves the department and outsources its services, the same activity (and, in many cases, the very same employees) are counted as 'services'.

In a word, the more competitive an economy becomes, the more important it is for everybody in it to become more and more efficient; and efficiency requires, first, correct allocation of resources. That such allocation is better delivered by market mechanisms than by planning bureaucracies is one of the few things in the world of economics and business for which there is not only a clear theory but also indisputable evidence.

Finally, technological trends that lower the cost of communications and information, may make it cheaper to coordinate across company boundaries rather than through bureaucracies.

Conclusion

Decisions made about vertical integration are extremely important, since they shape the company as much as or more than any decisions regarding the product. In reality there is a more marked difference between a manufacturer and a seller than between someone manufacturing for different markets. A car manufacturer and a refrigerator manufacturer are more similar than a refrigerator manufacturer and a chain of shops selling electrical goods. Furthermore, these decisions on integration are essential to establish a solid competitive position, either through exploiting the advantages or knowing how to retain a winning flexibility.

The analysis of the pros and cons must be careful, as it is quite easy to fall in to the trap of a number of false arguments, like those mentioned above. It is particularly important to remember that the margins made by suppliers (or buyers) cannot easily be taken over simply by integration, and that a supplier, because of its volume of production and experience, is often more cost-effective than an internal corporate division, although a superficial study may point to the contrary. It is also important to take into account some of the costs of integration that are usually overlooked. Together with this loss in efficiency you have got to remember the neglect of the company's basic activities (lack of specialization) and loss of flexibility (increase in fixed costs, 'technological paralysis') which integration frequently causes.

These considerations are particularly relevant to small and medium-sized companies that have limited resources and so need to specialize in a specific aspect of the business where they can quickly get to a certain level of production and technical capability that will put them in a comfortable competitive position. But this can only be achieved through the devotion of all management time and the company's limited financial resources to this area. For these companies integration certainly has many of the disadvantages of diversification, with the further problem that it would make them lose their flexibility, which, together with specialization is one of the best competitive weapons of small companies. Let us emphasize the point again: vertical integration although seeming to strengthen the company because it makes it bigger (it does more things 'internally') does not help at all to obtain economies of scale, since these usually come with a high volume of production at each stage of manufacture of the final product. The most direct method of obtaining economies of scale and so of being more competitive cost-wise is to specialize in a particular stage of the process and produce as much as possible there, instead of trying to 'do a bit of everything'. The next chapter is devoted to the study of such a strategy.

Reference

1 See Von Hippel, Erik, *User Innovation: An analysis of the functional sources of innovation*, Cambridge, Mass.: Sloan School of Management, Massachusetts Institute of Technology, 1985.

4 The fashionable mistake: over-subcontracting

Evidently all the problems associated with vertical integration and discussed in the previous chapter have not been missed by those companies suffering from them. As a result, in the last decade there has been a strong movement of vertical de-integration. Figure 4.1 shows the increase volume of sales per employee in the world's largest industrial companies.

This movement has taken many forms, from spinning off internal divisions to simply shutting down operations and switching to external suppliers. In any case this kind of subcontracting, understood here in a wide sense, has been seen by many executives as the appropriate way to 'restructure' their company. As in the case of vertical integration, if it

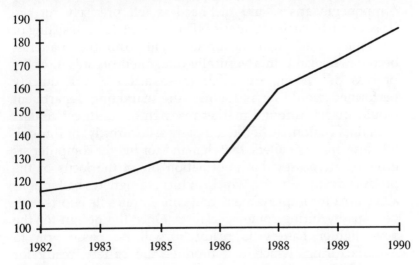

Figure 4.1 *Sales per employee in Fortune 500 companies*

may be true that subcontracting does indeed solve many of these problems, it is also true that it does not come without its drawbacks. In fact concerned voices have been raised in the last few years about the 'hollowing of the corporation',[1] the danger that, by subcontracting, the company may lose its 'essence' or, to use the fashionable expression, its 'core competences'.[2] This chapter will first look at the advantages of subcontracting as a means to organize the different activities of the business system, and then will turn to analyse why in many cases it is not the ideal solution, thus paving the way for the analysis, in the next chapter, of the 'third way'.

Advantages of subcontracting

An industry where most of the activities are carried out by independent companies, ones that contract as such with each other is simply an industry that follows market economics. Indeed capitalism is a system of allocating resources or, what comes down to the same thing, a means of coordinating activities, through more or less free market mechanisms.

Take the case of the computer industry we described in Chapter 2. If final users keep demanding ever lighter portable computers, the need to develop and manufacture ever lighter components arises, and the need is felt precisely for the heavier parts, such as batteries. Thus the activity consisting of designing and manufacturing light, durable batteries becomes relevant. In a vertically integrated organization the process of making sure that those activities are quickly performed would be as follows: the marketing department would detect, through market research or its direct contact with final customers (if the company sells directly) or through wholesalers or retailers, that demand for lighter computers is growing. It passes this information on to the locus of the product design activity, which, in turn, designates batteries as a key area for improvement, and concentrates its efforts in it, perhaps by hiring some specialists. Once the design for the new, lighter battery is ready, it will be passed on to manufacturing, which will produce the battery, ready for assembly into the new, improved model.

The market system is apparently simpler than that. Having sensed the need for lighter batteries, the computer assembler calls battery suppliers, demanding lighter batteries. These, sensing a need, design the new battery, and charge a better margin, for it is a novelty, which differentiates it, and will eventually differentiate the product assembled by the assembler. The high price being paid for the new battery is immediately a powerful signal for all people with the technical ability to develop a new battery that this is what they should be doing: that's where the money is right now. In the case of a vertically integrated company, somebody's decision that lighter batteries are important determine, in a hierarchical fashion, the work of designers. In the market system, it is the high price somebody is willing to pay that 'directs' designers to work in a specific direction.

Of course, in the second case, it is the designer of the lighter battery that keeps much of the value created for the final consumer (the reduced weight of the machine), while in the first case that value has remained 'in the company'. But, as we saw in the two previous chapters, the value is being created in the activity of designing (perhaps manufacturing) the batteries, and nowhere else. The market mechanism simply allocates the reward where the merit is, or, in strategic terms, makes it very clear where competitive advantages lies. As a result managers know directly which are the really profitable activities, and which are simply being 'carried' by them, because the intrinsic profitability of each activity (carried out by a different company) can be captured in a full profit and loss account.

In a way the difference between organizing the business system internally through vertical integration and doing it through subcontracting is not different from organizing the whole economy through central planning or through a market mechanism. Although there are very good arguments for coordinated central planning, reality has shown that letting the different players orient themselves by price signals simply generates much more wealth, for reasons now well understood. The parallel with the business system is not difficult to draw, as we saw in the previous chapter.

First, there is an issue of motivation. A subcontractor works for himself, and knows that any extra profits due to his efforts and innovativeness will accrue to him. This is the truer the smaller the subcontractor is, for the closer the ownership and direction of the company will be to the people actually performing the activity, down to being the same person. Conversely, the larger the company is, the less impact will the benefits make per person. Thus the engineers who have the know-how on light batteries will probably get the same salary as the others, blurring a powerful signal to direct bright people to work on what the company needs most.

Second, subcontracting resembles the market mechanism in that not all bets are placed on the same horses. Indeed one of the problems with central planning is that its efficiency is evidently dependent on the accuracy of the predictions on which the plans are based; and it doesn't take much argument to agree that our ability to predict future developments in most industries is, at best, limited. Thus a company that chooses, among several possibilities, the wrong technology, will perhaps be stuck with its decision for a long time. A company that subcontracts simply switches suppliers to those who have made the right technological bets.

Subcontracting appears also as a way to reduce costs, which is, interestingly, the opposite of the argument used by many defenders of vertical integration, as we saw in the previous chapter! That cost reduction may be achieved when performing the activity in-house implies operating at a less than efficient scale. By subcontracting one participates in the subcontractor's overall volume, which reduces costs by achieving an efficient scale. This is simply obvious in many cases, and is one of the reasons why companies never even think of subcontracting some of their operations (taxi fleets don't build their own cars).

Conversely, there are many activities for which there is a 'maximum efficient scale', i.e. there is a size *beyond which* costs go necessarily up. This is so because in any activity two costs have to be taken into account: those of actually producing the good or delivering the service, and those of managing the operation. Managing a large operation is more expensive, in different ways, than managing a small one. Of course the technological advantage of operating a large plant often more than compensates for the extra expense of managing a large unit. But in the absence of those advantages, a smaller unit is more efficient.

Thus the company can decide to subcontract an activity because it cannot achieve enough volume to do it efficiently, or for exactly the opposite reasons – because it is too large to match the costs of smaller operators. For many activities the decision is clear. But there are other cases where the limits are not so clearly defined. After all, as we know, the efficient scale for an activity is not etched in stone, and there is a margin in which reasonable doubt is possible. But in such cases, another reason may again tilt the scales the way of subcontracting: subcontractors may obtain lower costs if they specialize in the activity being subcontracted, which the subcontracting company by definition is not.

Organization experts talk about the 'cost of complexity'. It is well established by now that costs easily go up exponentially as one starts adding new products and activities. A subcontractor, by specializing in just one activity of the business system, is in a good position to produce at lower costs, even at the same volume, than is an integrated company, which has to divide its attention between several activities.

As we mentioned at the end of the previous chapter, there is a constant rise in the number of small businesses operating in our economies and, what is more interesting, in the number of people working in small businesses. There seems to be a strong trend toward subcontracting, both from the large companies restructuring, and from the views of many people that running their own business is a better way to control their future than traditional employment with a large organization. This motivation, discussed above, easily produces another important advantage: focused subcontractors can develop the 'industry culture' that facilitates efficient operations. In a large, integrated company the culture best attuned to its key competitive advantage is the one that eventually prevails, running the risk of imposing itself in other areas where is not the most suitable.

That 'culture' of course ends up having a large impact on efficiency. Thus we saw in the previous chapter how integrated companies can experience 'costs spill-over' from the more profitable activities into the rest of the business. If, in the absence of important barriers to entry, the activity being subcontracted allows for a relatively reduced margin, an independent subcontractor won't be able to charge more. An internal department, on the other hand, could impose company-wide high costs, developed under the protection of high barriers to entry to *another* activity.

An example is that of the new service being offered by AT&T. The company takes care of the '800 numbers' of its clients, i.e. when a customer calls Hewlett-Packard to get information on one of Hewlett-Packard's products, it is really an AT&T employee that answers the phone. The main reason why AT&T can offer a competitive price to its clients is that it has set up a brand new unit to do the work, one that uses unskilled, non-union personnel, with costs that reflect the reality of such a low value-added activity. Most of AT&T clients would have to treat those employees as though they were working in a high value-added business, which in reality they are not. In these cases (and there are many) subcontracting does indeed reduce costs.

These two factors (motivation and absence of 'spill-over' effects) come out as a key explanation of the success that many spun-off operations of large companies experience shortly after they are 'set free'. One of the latest cases is that of Lexmark, which was separated from IBM and in which was concentrated IBM's 'low margin' business in keyboards, typewriters, and printers. IBM still buys from it, and Lexmark uses the IBM brand, but its efficiency has increased dramatically: it has halved employment, been able to reduce debt dramatically, and has employees owning more than 15 per cent of the company's stock. This gap between the efficiency of an activity inside the company and the potential efficiency outside has created a good business opportunity for those who offer to 'take over' activities integrated companies were doing on their own. We just saw the example of AT&T's answering service, but whole computer departments are now being 'farmed out', as is hospital management.

We could summarize this section by saying that by letting a specialized, efficient-volume subcontractor perform the activity, a company can save money. ('Efficient' volume may be large or small, depending on the activity.) As we saw in the previous chapter, the margins of the subcontractor in themselves should not be a cause for concern: if they are low, let the subcontractor do it; if they are high, then . . . so will barriers to entry to the subcontractor's business be. The company must then decide whether it wants to jump over them, at the risk of losing focus and tying up resources that might be more profitably concentrated on other activities. If we add to these potential savings superior motivation and increased flexibility, it seems that subcontracting is exactly what the doctor ordered for the large, sometimes inefficient, integrated organizations.

But life within the business system is not as simple as that. Advantageous as it may be, subcontracting has some serious shortcomings that can render the practice highly damaging, as a host of companies have discovered in the last ten years. In the next section, we will see some of main problems presented by subcontracting, and will try to pinpoint their causes.

When subcontracting goes wrong

There are broadly speaking two main reasons why subcontracting may be dangerous. The first is intrinsic to the practice of subcontracting itself: if the company does not make the right decisions on what to do outside and what inside, it may find itself working on the 'wrong', i.e. least profitable, activities of the business system, even if at the beginning it does not look like that. The second kind of problem stems, at least partially, from the sets of solutions that companies have devised to deal with the first problem: by introducing protecting mechanisms, they end up raising costs system-wide, which render them eventually inefficient.

Intrinsic problems of subcontracting

One of the strongest criticisms that levelled against the practice of subcontracting is that it may end up by emptying the company of its contents, 'hollowing it out' – by subcontracting, the company lets outsiders capture key positions in the business system. Eventually the company finds itself squeezed out of the most interesting activities. This is indeed a serious charge, worth analysing in detail. To do that, we'll study an episode in the apparently never-ending saga of the assault on Western markets by Far Eastern competitors.[3]

The microwave oven has been, with the video cassette recorder, one of the very few domestic appliances to be introduced in the last twenty years. Surrounded by mature products, such as dishwashers or television sets, it became the 'star' in the planning departments of appliance manufacturers.

Although the product was invented in the USA, when a Raytheon technician noticed that his candy bar melted when working close to a microwave radar, the first companies to commercialize the oven in a big way were the large Japanese exporters of domestic appliances, particularly Matsushita, Sanyo and eventually Sharp. General Electric, however, entered strongly into the market, and by 1980 it had a 16 per cent market share, and finished a brand-new plant at Maryland devoted to the manufacture of its well-designed microwave ovens.

In 1983, however, GE's market share had dropped to 14 per cent. Although the market was still growing (7 million units were sold that year), customers were becoming a bit more price-conscious, and GE was having trouble matching the prices that were being offered by its Japanese competitors. As it is often the case, GE decided to explore the possibility of outsourcing at least some of the simplest models, where margins were thinnest.

GE's first thought of Matsushita, as world leader, by both volume and technology. In fact discussions were held with the Japanese, and pacts reached for some trial orders. But, understandably, GE's management was not too happy about subcontracting the whole manufacture of the oven to its main competitor – in that segment as in many others. It decided to look for alternatives.

It found one in Korea. A small but ambitious local company had just noticed how interesting the market for microwave ovens could be, and had entered the business by building a crude model, which it was exporting to Panama and to JC Penney in the US, to fill Penney's bottom of the line. Production was about 200,000 units per year, compared to the millions Matsushita was making. GE was surprised by the Korean company's low price, but did not trust such an unsophisticated company to supply the required top quality. After much effort on the part of the Koreans to gain the order, GE decided to maintain in-house manufacture of the top of the line, good-margin models, and to subcontract to Matsushita the production of the cheaper ovens, plus a small order of 15,000 units to the Koreans, to test them.

The first thing GE had to do, after placing the order, was to send a good number of American engineers to Korea to make sure that the standards of quality in an appliance that would bear the GE label would be maintained. Those engineers had to work hard with the Koreans who, besides a strong will to learn, had little else. Eventually hard work paid off, and the line started turning out acceptable ovens.

Gradually, GE increased its orders to Korea. Those ovens were working well, and the margin on them was far better than the margin on GE-built ovens. As price competition increased with the maturing of the market, cost considerations mattered more and more. At some point GE found itself with too little work for its specialized plant in Maryland: it had fallen below the minimum efficient scale. A decision had to be made between subcontracting the whole lot to Korea or building production in the US.

Managers in Maryland, faced with the alternative, made an astounding effort to design rationalization plans that would cut costs dramatically. But, even with those, the prices quoted by the Koreans were consistently lower. Facing strong competition, GE managers decided to go to the low cost supplier, and shut down the Maryland plant in May 1985.

The end of the story is not hard to guess. GE is out of the domestic appliances business altogether, and Samsung is the world's largest manufacturer of microwave ovens, having achieved that position in less than 10 years after entering the business with no technology, no expertise, no production lines, no marketing or distribution systems, and no brand name. How could Samsung do it?

Well, what is the best thing that could happen to a company like Samsung, willing to learn about a new and potentially profitable business, but about which it knew little? Obviously, that some of the masters would teach it, filling in for all its inadequacies. That is exactly what GE did. It taught Samsung quality control and American consumer requirements, assured them good volumes, so Samsung could go down the learning curve, and finally gave them international credibility by putting GE's label on their products, which facilitated penetrating other markets. In his wildest dreams Samsung's chairman could not have asked for more. Once Samsung knew how to manufacture top-quality, inexpensive ovens, it was a matter of time (and not too much, at that), until it could start selling, first in Europe, then everywhere, under its own brand name. After all, the most difficult part of making a microwave oven is . . . making a microwave oven. In this business, once that is achieved, the other 'activities' fall into place.

Let us try to draw general lessons from this story, in terms of the business system analysis we studied in Chapter 2. By subcontracting the manufacture of its ovens, GE chose to keep for itself those activities that were, long term, less attractive. There is no argument that in the short term a brand name in the domestic appliance business, and a distribution system such as GE had, are strong barriers to entry, ones that make the activity of marketing and distributing ovens potentially profitable. But that reputation is built on the actual ability to deliver good products, and that ability in this business belongs to the manufacturer. If a company is able to make the best value-for-money ovens, it is a matter of time (and willingness on its part) until it can start capturing most of the profits, either by gradually raising prices to customers (such as GE), which cannot make the ovens any more, or by 'integrating forward' and starting to sell direct, building its own brand and distribution system. In any case what looks *statistically* a profitable activity (marketing and distribution), becomes less attractive when the variable time is introduced.

This *dynamic* consideration of the effects of subcontracting on a company's position is essential, for it is in the nature of competitive advantage to be only temporary. Competitors rarely stand still, and it has been said that the only really sustainable competitive advantage is the ability to learn faster than anybody else, to add new competitive advantages as the old ones lose their profit potential. If that is so, consideration of each activity has to be made not only in terms of its intrinsic profitability today but in terms of how the profitability of the different activities chosen by the company will be affected by the choice itself. Again, the example of the computer industry shows why.

When IBM decided to enter the microcomputer market, it was in a hurry. The business had gone from being simply a hobbyist-controlled cottage industry to a supplier of useful tools for professionals (especially spreadsheets), something much closer to IBM's turf. The large company did not fail to see that the future of the whole computer industry might be somewhat affected by the arrival of those machines, and that it was therefore essential to be present as soon as possible in that segment.

Aware of its cumbersome product development practices, IBM decided to 'set this business free' by setting up a wholly decentralized operation in Southern Florida, in charge of designing, manufacturing and marketing IBM's entry into the personal computer arena. As we all know, to be as fast and flexible as possible, IBM decided to outsource the operating system to a tiny outfit called Microsoft and the micro-processor to one of the several producers, called INTEL. The design of the machine (specifications, circuitry, appearance) and the manufacture and distribution would be carried out by IBM itself.

If we go back to the business system of the industry as

outlined in Chapter 2, we realize that IBM decided to keep for itself precisely those parts of the system with the lowest intrinsic profitability: manufacture of standard memory chips, keyboards, assembly... The design is eminently copiable, and there is not a single piece of hardware that could command premium prices on its own, for, in order to be fast to market, IBM went for fairly standard, off-the-shelf components.[4]

Thus analysed, it is not surprising that IBM loses money today in its personal computer business. Although the company is apparently unable to provide completely reliable figures for each of its different businesses, industry analysts calculate that IBM lost about $1 billion in personal computers in 1992. As in the case of GE, IBM passed along the sustainably profitable activities of the system to its subcontractors. In this case those subcontractors didn't compete against IBM. They simply captured what could have been IBM's potential competitive advantage: to be the *de facto* standard setter, with the largest installed base.

It is, then, important to insist that the current mentality of many Western firms which, facing a strong assault on manufacturing, decide to concentrate on 'services' is highly dangerous. As we saw in Chapter 2, the idea that 'hardware is a commodity, software and services is where the money is' simply does not fit the evidence: together with Microsoft (software), Intel is the most profitable company in the business. Many distributors of personal computers, notably industry pioneers such as Businessland, have shut down. Most software manufacturers (word processors, spreadsheets, databases) have had to fold, facing ever stronger competition. Simultaneously, as we saw in Chapter 2, manufacturers of key components, such as ever lighter batteries and colour flat panel displays, enjoy above-average margins.

In addition to companies eventually giving away the best parts of the business, subcontracting has also the danger of cutting the company off from critical sources of learning. If, in order to ensure continued performance in one activity, one must be present in another, then the profits of the first activity are highly dependent on the second. Why could that happen? Because being active in one activity is in many cases the most efficient way to learn how to perform another activity better.

Take the case of innovation. It has been found that a huge proportion of all innovations introduced by companies are actually suggested by their customers.[5] If a company does not get direct access to them, it may find itself sticking to somebody's specifications, without the ability to bypass current state of the art and become a high margin innovator. Symmetrically, if the company sources a component that embodies the key technology, it will probably be in a weaker and weaker position *vis à vis* the supplier of that component, even if at the beginning it seemed to be well positioned, as we saw with GE.

Thus there are three risks to subcontracting: the company may transfer its competitive advantage to a subcontractor, which then becomes a successful competitor; the company can see its competitive advantage diffused to competitors by a common subcontractor; and the company may cut itself off from the sources of future innovation. In all three cases the company finds itself, at the end of the process, 'hollowed out'.

When subcontracting decreases individual costs and increases costs for the system

Many companies have been aware of these problems for years, and they have been in a position to avoid them, by instituting a number of practices that protect their competitive position from encroachment by their suppliers or customers. Those practices, however, have imposed a huge efficiency penalty, and, when new competitors have appeared that don't suffer from it, has made business as usual ('controlled subcontracting') impossible. The American automobile industry provides an outstanding example.[6] The following is a description of how the industry operated until the 1980s, when the wind of change became irresistible.

As is well known, a car manufacturer does not 'manufacture' that much – its main efforts are concentrated on designing the cars, down to each of the thousands of different pieces that make them up, and then assembling them. Much of the manufacturing is left to an army of subcontractors, which build the parts for the assemblers (known as OEMs in the industry). Thus, deciding which parts to give to subcontractors, which ones to keep in-house, and, what is more important, how to handle the subcontractors, are some of the most important decisions that the OEMs have had to take over the years.

The objective was quite clear: maximize the amount of profits in the manufacture of the car both today and in the future. This second point implies, as we saw in the example of GE, that the subcontractors do not end up 'owning' the OEM's sources of competitive advantage. The fact that none of the American subcontractors has ever been in a very strong position testifies, from the OEMs' point of view, the success of their strategy.

This strategy consisted essentially of the following points:

- First, the really key components of a car are never subcontracted. These components include the engine block, the transmission, and the main body panels. Producing those things is seen as the essence of being a car manufacturer.
- Second, never subcontract a complete 'system', i.e. a functioning, identifiable subset of a car, such as 'the brakes', 'the ignition', or even 'the seats'. OEMs subcontract only individual parts, which they will later on assemble. General Motors used as many as twenty-five different suppliers of parts for its seats, which it later assembled. Technical specifications for these parts were very strict, and not discussed with the suppliers but simply communicated.
- Third, for the parts being subcontracted, obtain as many suppliers (including the company's internal component divisions) as the minimum efficient scale for the component will allow. Thus if a piece can be efficiently

manufactured at a volume of 150,000 per year, and the company calculates it will need 500,000, it would usually make 200,000 in house and subcontract batches of 150,000 to two suppliers. This is the reason why General Motors ended up being both the most integrated of all Western manufacturers and the one that used the largest number of suppliers: its huge volume allowed it to do both things efficiently, i.e. always operating above the minimum efficient scale.

- Fourth, very rarely agree on contracts longer than a year.
- Finally, conduct the negotiating process as a public bid contest: give the specifications and volumes, and ask for prices. Those with the lowest prices get the business. Only companies with a track record in the industry need apply. If a supplier provokes an assembly line stoppage through failure of delivery or poor quality, it is immediately punished (its contract cancelled), and finds it difficult to win business again.

The philosophy behind these policies is not difficult to fathom: It is a matter of making sure that suppliers never develop enough 'car' expertise or even market differentiation to allow them to start demanding higher prices. If a supplier could, say, develop a reputation for making the safest brakes around, there is a chance that final customers might start valuing the incorporation of those brakes in the cars they bought. If that happened, it would not be too difficult for the supplier to demand higher margins, for it would really be contributing to the car differentiation. As a result, the system is designed to keep suppliers' margins down to the very minimum compatible with their continuing operation.

The reason subcontractors are used at all is to build in some flexibility: if final sales go down, suppliers make a nice 'buffer' before the OEM has to start cutting its own operations. Besides, given the right policies, their profitability would not be attractive anyway. It can be said that the OEM made sure that the activities in which the subcontractors were engaged did not have any chance to develop attractive profit potentials. The OEM kept the differentiation-building activities (design, engineering, key component manufacturing), and passed along the simplest things, such as individual part manufacturing, where the only value added is simple precision-machining to somebody else's specifications.

This way to organize the industry, led by General Motors, was the envy of the European manufacturers. In Europe manufacturers were much smaller, and suppliers relatively larger. Some of them could then impose their rules, and even have 'a life of their own': Bosch is an example of a company manufacturing full systems, such as electronic injection or ABS braking, with a unique technology that its customers (the European OEMs) had to buy in order to deliver quality to the final buyer of cars. In these circumstances it is not surprising that some of the European automobile suppliers have been more successful over the years than the OEMs. But the essence of the system was not very different; it was simply modified by the local circumstances.

As mentioned before, this way to coordinate the business system, based really on arm's-length market mechanisms, where prices are the only pieces of information that drive the behaviour of the economic actors, was successful in preventing the likes of General Motors from suffering a fate similar to that experienced by GE in domestic appliances or IBM in personal computers. If Western car manufacturers suffered mightily in the 1980s, it was certainly not because of their suppliers. As is well known, it was because of other competitors, which organized the business system in a very different way.

The mechanisms set up by car manufacturers to defend their competitive advantages added a number of significant costs to the system. As long as those costs were incurred by all competitors, their respective positions were sustainable. When a set of fresh competitors arrived, with a new, more efficient way of organizing the business system that did not contain those costs, the competitive position became untenable.

What are those costs? Think, for instance, of the impact on General Motors of some of its subcontracting practices. Take the refusal to subcontract complete sub-systems, such as brakes or seats, but only individual pieces. It forced GM engineers to design to the smallest detail every single piece of the car. This called for a huge army of engineers and designers, with all the problems associated with such a large operation. Second, the different pieces of a sub-system were often difficult to put together and work together: sometimes materials were incompatible, or the pieces were too difficult to assemble. By having farmed out production of the parts to independent companies, who did not talk to each other (they did not even know who was doing what), GM only discovered those problems at the very end, with the traditional delays and costs overruns.

The system did not allow for learning, either. Any improvement found by a subcontractor (a way, say, to increase quality or decrease costs) was jealously guarded, for it was a source of profits that would be quickly taken away if openly declared. When, on the other hand, there were quality or delivery problems, the car manufacturer did not work with the supplier to solve the problem (as GE engineers did with Samsung). Instead the faulty supplier was simply replaced. This was because suppliers would not dream of letting the manufacturer get inside their operations, for that would give the OEM the ability to assess the supplier's costs with even more precision, thus shaving the margins even further. And hiding its own costs was so important to the supplier, that many of them followed strategies of diversification just to make sure that no outsider would get a clear picture of the economics of their automobile business: diversified companies are not required to provide detailed information by line of business.

Even security of supply becomes expensive. The supplier knows that the worst sin it can commit is stopping the manufacturer's assembly line. Accordingly, it stores large amounts of finished parts, to make sure there will be no stockouts. But this has a cost, which necessarily gets built into the system. Shuffling those inventories from the OEM's plant (old system) to the supplier's (new system, under 'Westernized' just-in-time) does not change the financial expenses associated with carrying them. The system is just inefficient.

This is the crucial point. By minimizing costs in the different activities, the OEMs created huge costs in the required coordination (or, rather, lack of it) of these activities in order to deliver a finished car. It can be argued that introducing these costs was the price to pay to preserve their competitive advantages, and the example of GE in domestic appliances has shown that this might be true. But if the competitive advantage can be preserved without those costs, then the resulting final car will be a winner. This is, of course, what some Japanese competitors did. But we will study that in the next chapters, for they did it precisely by moving away from both vertical integration and market-based sub-contracting.

Conclusions

Subcontracting seems for many reasons to be the way the world is going. It fits well the need to de-layer large companies, to put those who have to perform the job really in charge of it. It helps take advantage of superior competence and more efficient technology. Finally, it solves the problems of 'cost spill-over', thus making sure efficient companies stay that way, and opens up ways to be ever more flexible.

But it does not come free. By subcontracting, companies run serious strategic risks, if performing the activities that are being subcontracted has an important bearing on how competitive the company will be in the activities it keeps in-house. Protecting itself against those dangers is possible, but it may entail serious costs, which are then added to the system. In essence, it can be said that coordinating the different activities of the business system, particularly from a dynamic perspective, is expensive both through vertical integration and through subcontracting. In some cases one of the two solutions is clearly adequate. But in many others none is fully satisfactory. If a way can be found to maintain maximum efficiency in the activities and lower coordination costs, that way will become the organization of choice, and companies adopting that organizational form will beat vertically integrated and market-based competitors. That organizaational form I called strategic network in Chapter 1, and is the topic of the rest of this book.

References

1 See Mark Pastin, 'The Hollow Corporation', *Executive Excellence*, vol. 5, 1988.
2 See C.K. Prahalad and Gary Hammel, 'The Core Competences of the Corporation', *Harvard Business Review*, May–June 1990.
3 For a more detailed account, see Magaziner, Ira C and Mark Patinkin, 'Fast Heat: How Korea Won the Microwave War' *Harvard Business Review*, January–February 1989.
4 For technical accuracy, we may say that IBM did keep a small part of the operating system proprietary, imbedded in a custom-made chip, called the BIOS (basic input-output subroutines). But it was small enough so that a couple of small upstart companies could 'reverse engineer' it and sell it in the open market for a low price and a good margin.
5 See Von Hippel, Erik, *User Innovation: An analysis of the functional sources of innovation*, Cambridge, Mass.: Sloan School of Management, Massachusetts Institute of Technology, 1985.
6 For more data, see James P. Womach, Daniel T. Jones and Daniel Roos, *The Machine That Changed The World*, New York: Rawson Associates, 1990; also Clark, Kim and Takahiro Fujimoto, *Product Development Performance*, Boston: Harvard Business School Press, 1991.

5 The emerging solution: the strategic network

In this chapter we get to the core of the problem. How can a whole business system be organized so that it has (most of) the advantages of vertical integration *and* subcontracting, without (most of) its drawbacks?

Understanding how a strategic network works is not easy, for most of its key features are, as we will see, counter-intuitive. For this reason, I shall explain in copious detail how one such network operates, to provide the background against which we can understand the essence of coordination through networking. We shall see how a small sweater-knitting operation turns into one of the world's most successful apparel companies, while in the process changing the way the industry operates. To balance that one example, we shall also discuss the way Japanese automobile manufacturers deal with their subcontractors. The contrast with the traditional (now somewhat changed) Western way that we saw in the previous chapter will help clarify the concept of strategic network, thus paving the way for the next part of the book, where a general theory of strategic networks is drawn – their essence, when they the most efficient way to do business, how one such network can be set up, how it can be maintained, how it can be expanded.

Benetton S.p.A.

The Benetton story,[1] if not exactly one of rags to riches, is nevertheless a tale of huge success built from humble origins. Started some thirty years ago, the company reached almost £2 billion worldwide sales by 1993, building from its strengths in one of the most mature, labour-intensive industries in labour-expensive Western Europe.

Luciano Benetton was born in 1935, and his childhood coincided with the harsh times brought to Northeastern Italy by the Second World War. Upon his father's death he had to leave school at the age of 15 to take a job in a men's clothing store. In 1955 Luciano, who had just turned 20, put into operation the first of the simple, daring schemes that were to make his fortune. He told his sister Giuliana he was convinced that he could market the brightly-coloured original sweaters she had continued to make as a hobby, so why shouldn't they leave their jobs and start a business?

With 30,000 lire, obtained from the sale of Luciano's accordion and his brother Carlo's bicycle, Luciano and Giuliana bought a knitting machine, and soon afterward Giuliana put together a collection of eighteen pieces. Luciano was immediately able to sell them to local stores. Sales increased steadily over the next few years, until Giuliana had a group of young women working for her. Luciano had bought a minibus to carry these employees to and from a small workshop the Benettons had set up near their home.

In the early 1960s, Luciano Benetton put into practice several innovative but thoroughly practical ideas that helped turn the company from a small enterprise into a giant. The first idea was to sell only through specialized knitwear stores (as opposed to department stores and boutiques selling a wide range of clothes), whose owners would presumably be more interested in pushing sales of his particular product. At that point Benetton sweaters did not bear the family name (they used foreign names, such as 'Lady Godiva' or 'Très Jolie'), but they already had the Benetton characteristics of medium-high quality and stylish design at a very reasonable price.

Two more new ideas emerged, this time for lowering production costs. The first was a novel technique for making wool soft, like cashmere; it was based on a method Luciano had observed while visiting factories in Scotland, where rudimentary machines with wooden paddles beat raw wool in water. The other idea was to buy and adapt obsolete hosiery-knitting machines, at a price of £5,000 apiece, a fraction of the cost of a new machine. The refurbished machines did their new job perfectly, and Benetton soon opened a gleaming new factory in Ponzano Veneto, a few kilometres outside Treviso. As in all his other activities, Luciano took a lot of care to give the factory the most modern look possible, by commissioning a couple of architects who were eventually to design his stores also.

As as we have seen, Luciano was always concerned by both the creation of original sweaters *and* the way they reached the public. Contrary to industry norms, he didn't think his job ended when selling his clothes to some wholesaler. He always wanted to reach the final customer direct. In 1968 the company opened the first independent outlet in the mountain village of Belluno, again not far from Venice. With its appealing merchandise and its spare, intimate interior, the shop was an immediate success. The store occupied only about 40 m², in part because of limited Benetton product line at the time, but it set the pattern for the stores to follow. As Luciano himself said later, 'It was conceived on the idea of the specialized store, the desire for an alternative to the department store. From the beginning, we wanted to create an image – the right people to open our stores, the décor, the colours.'[2]

Through the late 1960s and early 1970s the Benettons concentrated their efforts on capturing the domestic market. By 1975 the distinctive white and green Benetton knitting-stitch logo, designed by Franco Giacometti – a long-time friend and associate of Luciano's – had become the symbol of a phenomenon in the Italian commercial scene. Approximately 200 Benetton shops had opened in Italy in 5 years, in a business where such 'chains' were completely unheard of.

Although it had opened an 'image-building' store in Paris in 1969, the company remained essentially Italian until the early 1980s: in 1979, 98 per cent of the company's sales of £80 million were in Italy. Then the company embarked on a strong internationalization effort, based partly on the notoriety they got by having young, glamorous women such as Princess Diana or Caroline of Monaco wearing the company's clothes.

The speed of the expansion was remarkable: 2000 shops were opened in Europe in just three years, quadrupling sales to £351 million by 1983. By the end of 1985 Benetton reported 3200 shops in fifty-seven countries. One year later the company had nearly 4000 shops all over the world, including 800 in the USA, a few stores in Eastern European countries and even three shops in Lebanon, then in the middle of its civil war. Exports represented more than 60 per cent of sales. Today the company has sales of more than US$ 2 billion per annum, in more than 6000 shops, in more than forty countries.

Of course, as the company grew, the Benettons had to hire professional managers. The Benetton siblings sat on the board of directors, but did not play the traditional role of members of the board. They took part in many day-to-day decisions, to the point that most of the senior functional managers had two reporting relationships: a formal one to the newly appointed professional general manager (whose previous job was with the Bank of Italy) and an informal one to a member of the Benetton family.

Today Benetton is probably the world's best known apparel company. Its size gives it enough volume to justify extensive marketing campaigns, sponsoring of Formula 1 teams, etc., all expenditures that few of its smaller competitors can afford. But its pervasive concern with 'image' has also made its 'advertising dollar' go longer. From the original way of setting its colourful shop windows (now imitated by most competitors), to advertising campaigns with shocking images, and Luciano Benetton's (now elected a senator in Italy) showing up naked in all the world media, asking for clothes for the needy, the company makes its presence felt, in a world (fashion) where presence is absolutely necessary.

Interesting as Benetton's success may be, however, what matters to us of course is *how* it was achieved. After all, as we mentioned, the Benettons did not 'invent' anything, or take advantage of special local conditions, to prosper in an extremely mature, low-growth industry. Their *real* innovations are to be found in their strategy and in the way they organized their company, and the companies around them, to implement that strategy.

A network organization

Luciano Benetton has always defined his company's strategy as developing 'industrial fashion', as opposed to the 'artisan' level of the rest of Italian fashion. He focuses the firm on the youth segment, middle income, with a strong global outlook. Let us look at the implications of that strategy.

* To be successful in the 'fashion' business, a company needs constant adaptation to its targeted group's tastes. It also needs to keep in extremely close contact with its customers, and provide a fast response to changes. For both these things it must have fast feed-back circuits.
* Being 'industrial' means the pursuit of volume, with all the attendant economies of scale. This, in turn, will give it the possibility of offering good design and very good quality at moderate prices.
* Finally, the global outlook is in fact required by the two preceding goals. It is necessary to obtain economies of scale (industrial advantages), but it is also perceived as a strength by the customer group (fashion appeal).

Of course, there is some *prima facie* contradiction between these points; fashion has always been considered artisan, more than industrial, and it could be argued that its industrialization would kill its fashion appeal and ability to respond to shifting tastes. In a word, how can you plan and still be flexible? For similar reasons, it could be said that a truly global outlook goes against the necessary adaptation to different tastes throughout the world. Thus the strategy sounds interesting, for 'fashion' conjures high prices, and 'industrial' low costs but . . . how can it be done? As we shall see now, it is the Benetton structure, the way it organizes the whole business system that lets it get away with the best of all worlds.

Benetton is a vertically de-integrated company, not only in manufacturing, but also in the other activities that make up the business system it moves in: styling and design, manufacturing, logistics and distribution, and sales. The company relies on external people and companies for the major part of these crucial activities. For sales of US$2 billion, it only employed directly about 1000 people in 1992.

The styling or design of the garments is done outside the company by a number of international free-lance stylists. Giuliana Benetton, with a staff of about twenty in the Product Development Department, interprets the 'look' created by the stylists and performs the modelling phase.

More than 80 per cent of manufacturing is done outside the company, by 350 subcontractors, which employ more than 10,000 people. In-house production accounts for the remaining less than 20 per cent (mostly dyeing) and is performed by 700–800 people. Logistics and distribution activities are also performed mainly by outsiders, who deliver the finished garments direct to every shop in the world.

Finally, the company uses an external sales organization of about 100 agents that takes care of a retailing system of 6000 shops spread all over the world. The internal part of this activity is performed by a reduced number of area managers, who coordinate the selling system by territories.

All these arrangements give the company an amazing degree of both flexibility and ability to plan ahead. The Benetton operating cycle consists of two fashion seasons: spring/summer, beginning in February and ending in July, and fall/winter, beginning in September and ending in December. The large volume of business done by the company requires that production planning for woollen and cotton articles begins far in advance of shipment to the stores. Roughly 21 months elapse from the preparation of clothing designs for a particular selling season to the final payment of commissions to Benetton agents.

Basic steps in the operating cycle are as follows: preparation of final designs; assembly of a few samples of each of the 600 items in the total collection; a 'pre-presentation' meeting with manufacturing managers and some of the company's 100 agents, which eliminates about a quarter of the items; producing the remainder in small quantities for presentation by area managers to agents and by agents to store owners; 'exploding' a rough production plan for the season, by fabrics and styles; making purchases according to that plan, and negotiating capacity with the subcontractors; finally starting production and beginning deliveries just in time for the selling season. Deliveries are scheduled so that each store can present 80 per cent to 90 per cent of all items in the collection to Benetton's customers at the outset of the selling season.

Thus Benetton, unlike most competitors, works only on firm orders for final shops, not for wholesalers or other intermediaries. But it retains a high degree of flexibility: the basic production plan is adjusted regularly through the presentation of a 'flash collection' just before the season. This flash collection corrects styling mistakes in the basic product line and usually includes about fifty new designs based on 'hit styles' presented by fashion houses (competitors) during the two main seasonal shows.

Orders can also be adjusted through 're-assortment', which is perhaps the most critical phase in the production plan, requiring great coordination and follow-through by retailers, agents and producers. Re-assortment occurs during the last third of each selling season, when retailers are allowed to add orders to their original ones based on sell-through of popular items. Juggling retail orders to match manufacturing capacity for thousands of shops in a five-week period is not an easy task. There is obviously a minimum economical production batch, so sometimes when the re-assortment order is not enough to fill the minimum batch, the marketing people have to get in touch with shop managers to propose some alternatives. In the last few years, as Benetton has moved into new geographic areas, the complexity of re-assortment has increased, because the best sellers for different areas tend to vary widely.

Manufacturing activities

The company is divided into three divisions: wool, cotton, and jeans. In 1983 Benetton had seven plants in Italy. In 1985 the number of plants fell to five, and after 1987 the company owned just three production units, one for each division. The reason for this reduction in the number of plants is simply a matter of the company's philosophy of vertical de-integration and external production as a mode of organization. All those divested plants act now as Benetton-exclusive sub-contractors.

The wool division works with less than ten suppliers of raw materials. Benetton is the biggest purchaser of wool thread in the world – more than 9 million kilos per year. The other two divisions buy raw materials (fabrics) from eighty to ninety different suppliers. The company centralizes all the purchasing activities, as this is perhaps the main source of economies of scale in the industry. To give an idea of the magnitudes involved, in 1987, 37 tonnes of yarn and 40 tonnes of fabrics entered the production system daily, to be transformed into 180,000 garments, adding up to 40–45 million garments per year.

Once the raw materials are in, Benetton turns to a small army of 350 subcontractors for actual production. Benetton gives these external contractors the exact amount of raw materials (calculated by computer), technical documents, an idea of the time needed to perform each single production activity, etc. Therefore, although these production units are external, Benetton provides much of the technical ability to run them. In addition, it advises subcontractors about the required machinery to buy, and offers them financial aid through its own leasing and factoring companies. The contact with the subcontractors is also facilitated because practically every Benetton manager is at the same time owner, president, or director of a leading subcontracting company in the system.

Even allowing for the added costs of shuttling raw materials and semi-finished products among subcontractors and Benetton's factories, total production costs for woollen items are almost 20 per cent below those of garments of comparable quality made in Europe and on a par with those made in the Far East. To understand how that impressive efficiency is achieved, we have to look carefully at the way the company is run. A close inspection of the wool division's production system will explain it. That division represents about 50 per cent of the company's operations. Its production process consists essentially of four sequential phases: knitting, assembling, dyeing, and finishing.

Knitting

The proportion of internal work in the knitting phase has been decreasing steadily. In 1982, only 40 per cent of the knitting of wool had been performed externally. As shown in Table 5.1, just 1 per cent of the knitting phase was done internally in 1987, and 90 per cent of that 1 per cent was concentrated in a very specific type of knitting machine. Benetton had decided to keep in-house that kind of machine, because it had a lot of problems finding it in external companies. That machine was very expensive, and therefore risky for external contractors. The company also used its internal production to gain an idea of the productivity and costing of the knitting phase.

Benetton works with seventy to eighty subcontractors in the knitting phase, and nearly 90 per cent of them work

Table 5.1 *Summary chart of the manufacturing process in the wool division*

Production phase	Per cent performed externally	Number of contractors	Degree of exclusiveness (%)
Knitting	99	70–80	90
Assembling	100	100	100
Chemical treatment	70–75	3	100
Dyeing	0	0	0
Finishing	95	20	100

exclusively for Benetton. The company asks for exclusivity so that it can plan its production, as it knows the subcontractors' production capacity, kinds of machine, number of shifts, etc. In exchange of course the company is expected to assure the saturation of their machines, which is risky for both Benetton and the external contractors.

Assembly

This phase of the manufacturing process is performed outside the company. In the early 1980s about half the assembly was still carried out in-house, but by the end of the decade all of it had been externalized to more than 100 exclusive subcontractors. Most of those employ less than fifteen staff, for Italian laws call for greater regulation of business above that size. Fourteen people are also an efficient number to run a garment assembly line.

The company feels that there are some economies in doing this job externally, because these small subcontractors have to pay less in terms of social costs according to Italian law, although the salary level is almost the same as it would be within Benetton. In addition, these small workshops reach a higher productivity than larger subcontractors, because of tighter control exercised by the owner. This last reason is the most important to Benetton, and it reflects the existence of diseconomies of scale in a phase that is labour-intensive.

Dyeing

The early 1970s saw the development of Benetton's perhaps most widely publicized production technique: the dyeing of assembled garments rather than yarn, for single-colour garments. Up to then it was the yarn that was dyed, and then the parts knitted and the sweater assembled. The Benettons discovered that, to some extent, the critical fashion factor was colour, not shape. Thus they would knit and assemble a large part of their production undyed ('grey') and wait until fashion trends for colours became clear to make the final colour decision. They thus avoided overproduction of sweaters in non-appealing colours and ensured they could meet demand for the 'best hits' of the season. The process was slightly more expensive but had the advantage of allowing production to respond quickly to public demand. It also allowed the company to maintain almost no inventory, and to produce mainly to order. The importance of this technique, however, should not be exaggerated: it can only be applied to knitwear of one solid colour. As soon as the sweater has several colours, it has to be knit with the coloured threads.

Contrary to what happens in the rest of the division, the company keeps 100 per cent of the dyeing phase internally. Curiously, it started the other way around: in 1982, half this phase was performed outside the company. The reason for concentrating the whole process at home was the great importance of the dyeing phase for a company whose main distinctive product characteristic was its colourful style. In addition, dyeing is both the most complex and the most capital-intensive process, which makes it risky for external subcontractors. Capital requirements for this phase are relatively high, well over £3 million. As this is one of the sources of competitive advantage for Benetton, the company feels it is too risky to leave it in subcontractors' hands, because they could use this process to sell to competitors, too.

Before the dyeing phase, every article has to pass through a chemical treatment to soften and wax the wool. The pieces that use already coloured threads had to pass through this chemical treatment, too. This phase is also a capital intensive one, but, technically speaking, is not as sophisticated as dyeing. The main part of this chemical process (70–75 per cent) is performed by three external companies. Two of these plants had belonged to Benetton until 1985, when it sold them to their plant managers. These plants became joint ventures between these new entrepreneurs and Benetton. Financial reasons (freeing resources for other activities) and manufacturing reasons (productivity and flexibility) had made it advisable to de-integrate the chemical treatment phase. The plants employ about 100 people each.

Finishing

Only 5 per cent of this phase is performed in-house, in contrast to the 80 per cent performed internally in 1982. The twenty subcontractors that perform the other 95 per cent work exclusively for Benetton. This phase is labour-intensive and does not require particular machinery. It is split into two parts: on-line quality control of each single article and packaging.

Arrangements in other divisions are very similar. In general, manufacturing operations are subcontracted, with a few exceptions. One is computer-aided design, where computers prepare the digital information to be used for the numeric control knitting machines used by all subcontractors, linked to Apricot computer aided design personal computer terminals. Designers using the CAD terminals play around with knitwear colours and patterns on a video screen. Once a designer decides on a particular pattern, the knitting machine automatically produces the fabric, usually in the easy-to-assemble form of pattern pieces.

Benetton was very early, too, in adopting sophisticated cutting technology: a laser system, linked to a CAD-CAM unit, cuts the fabrics in an optimal fashion, in shapes that come straight from the designers' screens. The CAD-CAM system's automatic cutter follows pattern pieces stored in the computer's memory, and turns out 15,000 full garments every 8 hours, wasting less than 15 per cent of the cloth.

Evidently being a Benetton subcontractor is no easy task. They must be ready to accept a great number of changes in articles, colours, etc., and do so in a very short time. They must adjust their machines weekly or even nightly to follow all these changes. This means a large number of different articles produced in small batches each, which, from a manufacturing point of view, is relatively inefficient. But they understand that that is part of the price they have to pay to adjust to Benetton's strong marketing outlook.

Working exclusively for Benetton has its risks, but it has the advantage of allowing subcontractors to dispense with a sales and marketing department. In the words of one of those subcontractors, 'The constant work provided by Benetton enables this company to concentrate on manufacturing, with just a few people in charge of administrative and financial tasks. Working only for Benetton means one invoice per month, fixed payment conditions, etc. We often receive requests from potential clients, but I would rather work this way.'

Subcontractors work normally 8 hours a day, but when the company is in a hurry they have to work over the weekend, and 12 or more hours a day. Nearly 10 per cent of all subcontractors are released every year because they do not meet quality standards.

But those subcontractors are not left alone. Benetton maintains a sort of 'umbilical cord' with external contractors. Plant managers know each subcontractor and some of them are personal friends, to the extent that the subcontractors talk to them about their problems and ask for advice. Manufacturing people visit subcontractors frequently. In addition, they are permanently in touch by phone. This daily communication allows them to work in real-time, solving small problems and making production adjustments.

According to Benetton, the less experienced the subcontractor in the apparel industry, the better it adjusts to Benetton's philosophy. It feels it is more difficult to create this umbilical cord with people that have previously worked for other clients. The experienced contractor tries to impose its conditions before starting the relationship.

Finally, there is a sort of strong identification with Benetton, not only within the company, but also among subcontractors' employees. They feel very proud of belonging to a world-wide-known group born in an ignored province of Italy.

Advantages of subcontracting

Benetton obtains very clear advantages over what internal production could offer:

- *Extreme flexibility*: when the firm must produce more than expected of a certain item, because fashion so demands, subcontractors can easily work extra time or over week-ends. That would be very difficult for a company with more than 10,000 workers, most surely unionized (that is what Benetton would be if it were vertically integrated). This flexibility is crucial to a fashion firm. Benetton is able to 'restock' its shops in mid-season thanks to this extremely flexible system.

- *Very low costs*: in labour-intensive, low-qualification opera-tions (such as garment assembly), close supervision is essential to obtain labour productivity. There is no closer supervision than ownership of a family business with no more than fourteen employees (the case for most assem-blers). In other operations the constant effort by hundreds of small entrepreneurs to find ways to cut costs is the best way to productivity. This is especially so in a field where cost containment comes more frequently from 'clever ideas' than from technological breakthroughs. It is impor-tant to realize that, in any case, subcontracting is not a way to reduce salaries, but overheads, and to improve efficiency.

Thus its original arrangements with suppliers give Bene-tton a clear edge over competitors. But this is only half (or actually less) of the story. To understand Benetton's success we must look at the whole business system, from raw material purchasing to actual delivery of the finished product to the final customer. This takes us into the 'downstream' part of Benetton: its distribution system.

Selling activities

There are three groups of actors engaged in selling activities: the company, the agents, and the shop owners and managers. The agents constitute the interface between Benetton and the shops. Twice a year all agents spend a week at headquarters getting to know the new collection for the season and selecting a sample of 30–40 per cent of the 600 items in the total collection. After this every agent goes back to his territory and takes about 30 or 40 days to visit and present the sample collection to each shop owner. Then the agent helps the shop owner in selecting the most suitable articles for each particular shop, and asks for orders. At the end of each day the agent sends the orders collected that day to headquarters, specifying the quantity, designs, colours, sizes, etc. Articles are shipped direct to the shops from the central warehouse, without passing through the agent. The shop owner sends the money direct to Benetton, after which the company pays the agent a 4 per cent commission on the value of goods shipped from the factories.

The agents, shop owners and managers are not Benetton employees, though Luciano Benetton personally has hand-picked most of the agents. A prospective agent's friendship with the Benetton family and reliability tend to outweigh the highlights of a resumé or experience in the apparel industry. Benetton's relation with agents has been managed largely on a verbal basis of trust: only since 1984 have formal contracts begun to be exchanged between Benetton and the agents. (Shop owners continue to have no legal contract with agents or with the company.) Agents have rarely had to be replaced for failure to meet expectations. Since they earn 4 per cent on the value of goods sold to the shops, most agents have ended up earning more money than any executive at Benetton, including the managing director. Agents who make a lot of money have been strongly encouraged to use part of their newly found capital to open new shops.

Selection of the agents is critical. Luciano Benetton deliberately looked for people without experience in the apparel distribution business. He was more interested in candidates with an enthusiastic predisposition towards the work itself, people who could be potential consumers rather than agents, who could understand the product – the multicoloured sweater, which back in the early days was completely unconventional – and believe in it. At the beginning most of the agents were Luciano's friends, and they preferred to report to him rather than to professional managers. They felt more committed to the owner than the company. Although the company has grown very large, it still uses the same criteria for choosing an agent: young people, very enthusiastic about work, who understand the product, like it, and believe in it. An executive of the company put it this way: 'The thing that really strikes Luciano Benetton is the entrepreneurial spirit in an agent, rather than anything else.'

The main responsibilities of the agents are:

(a) To present the collection to shop managers and help them in choosing goods.
(b) To collect orders and transmit them to headquarters.
(c) To find and select potential investors for new shops.
(d) To select the location of new shops.
(e) To help new clients in starting shops and train them, usually in the agent's.
(f) To look after the shops and help clients to manage and control them.
(g) To encourage image competition among shops. Agents were also encouraged to reinvest part of their commissions in opening new shops, thus becoming clients themselves. This policy of encouraging agents to have and run their own shops helps them to get a first-hand knowledge of the retail business and its problems in practice.

Agents normally have a small organization to help them perform their multiple activities. Although agents visit the shops regularly, they usually hire young assistants to control the shops' image and problems on a weekly basis. In addition, the assistants help the agent in the task of monitoring the new trends in young's people culture. They have to visit the places where they meet (discotheques, bars, etc.) and see how they behave, not only what they wear.

Agents train their assistants in their own shops. This training period is critical for assistants in order to learn the mechanics and operating problems of running a shop. Training focuses on marketing aspects (how to sell, how to improve the service, how to train and manage salespeople) and layout aspects (how to display the garments, how to dress the window, what is the right music).

Shop operations

Retailers very often were chosen in the same way. As Luciano Benetton put it, 'We have caused a new type of retailer to become important who until the day before was perhaps a florist or a hairdresser. His prior career was of no importance, but he had to have the right spirit to work in a Benetton shop.' Those owners do not sign franchise agreements (Luciano Benetton hates bureaucracy and finds that the current arrangement 'stimulates the full capacity of the owners'). They are neither required to pay Benetton a fee for use of its name nor a royalty based on a percentage of sales or profits. Therefore the term 'franchising' in describing the Benetton retailing network is really a misnomer. Store owners, among other things, are required to carry only Benetton merchandise, maintain a minimum sales level, adhere to suggested mark-ups of about 80 per cent from cost, pay for their orders within 90 days and, the most important thing, develop an understanding of Benetton's way of doing business.

Fewer than ten of the Benetton stores worldwide are owned and operated by the company. These are located in key cities such as Milan, New York, Rome, and Düsseldorf. Benetton has found little difficulty in getting entrepreneurs all over the world to invest between £10,000 and £300,000 per shop. Benetton approves the location of the shops and Luciano personally still oversees the more strategic sites.

According to the garments sold in them, the interiors and exteriors of the shops, generally in vivid green, must be decorated in the Benetton style, with the appropriate furniture, colour of lighting, type of music, and appropriate sex, age, and dress style for salespeople. All these elements have been studied and selected to attract the targeted clientele. Shops are also required to follow basic merchandising concepts, the most important among them being that all merchandise must be displayed on open shelves accessible to customers, who can touch it and try it on. The open displays in an otherwise undecorated space create an impression of great colour and fashion to the window-shopping customer.

Shop owners are not retail experts. Mr. Weiss, area manager

for North America, Japan and Eastern Europe, commented, 'Experts in retailing are not good shop owners (and managers) because they do not understand very well the particular Benetton system.' When asked about this 'system', he mentioned the following characteristics:

(a) New window display every week.
(b) Good salespeople in stores, good service.
(c) Competition of image among shops (window decoration, garments diversity and display).
(d) 150 items per shop.
(e) No price competition.
(f) Initial prices set at factory or 'suggested' (US case).
(g) Markdowns discussed with agents.

Benetton uses five mechanisms to control its 'identity' in spite of the dramatic increase in the number of shops:

- Standardization of the shop image. Retailers have to choose among twelve basic layouts and fixture selections. Furniture must be provided by only three Italian suppliers, located near headquarters.
- Central supply of advertising material, which is produced at headquarters and shipped to the shops all over the world. Shops are allowed to do some advertising in local media (mainly newspapers) after the company has checked the advertisement.
- A strict pricing policy. The computer back at Benetton prints the price in local currencies on each tag attached to every article. For the US market it is a 'suggested' price.
- Benetton shops can only sell Benetton products.
- Assistance to new clients.

Standard expenses of a normal shop are: 10 per cent lease, 9–12 per cent salaries, 3 per cent general expenses, 4 per cent legal fees (credit cards, etc.) and 2 per cent electrical expenses. Shops normally obtained a 45–50 per cent gross return on their investment.

Advantages of shops

Its shops are crucial to Benetton's success, for it tries to provide a 'complete fashion package', and the sales point is an integral part of it. Benetton shops have their own 'character', which not only consists of the décor but also of the eagerness and ability of the salespeople to help customers match different garments to obtain a coordinated 'ensemble' that is fashionable. They do this extremely well. It is impossible to enter a Benetton store asking for a sweater without being immediately offered shirts, slacks and even socks that go perfectly with it. It is very difficult to buy just one garment, because the Benetton collection fits together so well and because the shop attendants make sure the customer realizes it, by giving valuable advice.

This 'network' of shops provides Benetton with the following advantages over company-owned stores:

- The shops being service businesses, where customer contact is paramount, they benefit greatly from very close owner supervision (this is standard 'doctrine' in most franchising operations, and there is plenty of empirical evidence to prove its efficacy).
- The necessary level of motivation from the salespeople is also easier to get if the head clerk is the owner's daughter or son, as is often the case, or if the attendants have expectations of improving their position as the owner's own chain grows, or even to set up their own shops.
- Benetton's speedy development of a web of shops throughout the world would have been impossible without a high level of local expertise.

The essence of the system

Benetton has achieved simultaneously the goals of outstanding efficiency, flexibility, and ability to innovate, and in those points rests its success. The brilliant colours of its sweaters can be (and have been) quickly copied by competitors. A system that consistently delivers products at 20 per cent lower costs than those of comparable goods cannot fail. That efficiency is achieved through having the right size for each activity (huge purchasing, tiny knitters), keeping each unit focused on its activity, with its own culture, and maintaining a high degree of entrepreneurial motivation. In a way Luciano Benetton has something that anybody would love to have – about 4000 entrepreneurs, i.e. people who by definition only work for themselves, working for him. If motivation is important (and it is crucial in small, labour intensive units, as it is in customer oriented shops), then his system will have a huge built-in advantage over an integrated company.

But de-integration is not enough. Efficiency as well as flexibility demand that the system be run as a whole unit. If Benetton went for the typical arm's length relationships we discussed in the previous chapter, many of the things that are crucial to its success could simply not be done, from planning in advance, knowing that all production capacity is always available, to lowering system costs by preventing every subcontractor from having to have a sales operation. Part of Benetton's efficiency and flexibility (think of the fastest turnaround time in the industry!) is explained by it being made up of many small units, and part is explained by being a large, homogeneous system. A pure web of arm's-length subcontractors could not deliver with the flexibility and efficiency that the Benetton *system* achieves.

That flexibility, as well as Benetton's uncanny ability to remain in touch with its markets (its ability to learn), is also made feasible by it being present throughout the business system, from raw materials to final sales. If Benetton sold in a more 'typical fashion', i.e. to wholesalers and large department stores, there is no way the firm could 're-assort' shops of exhausted, top-selling items, within the same season. Again, a purely de-integrated system would not do. An integrated operation with thousands of company-owned small shops is probably out of the question. How many layers of supervision and control, for example, would such an operation demand? In the Benetton system just one layer, the agents, and they don't even belong to the company!

Thus Benetton achieves most of the advantages of vertical integration – planning, direct coordination, unity of purpose, no need to constantly renegotiate – and also captures the advantages of subcontracting – most efficient size for each activity, maximum motivation, ability to respond quickly to special demands. Going back to the vocabulary of the previous chapters, we can conclude that the Benetton system delivers the final goods most efficiently because each of the activities in the system is performed most efficiently. But, even more important, the coordination costs of the whole operation are also managed in the most efficient way. It is not surprising, as we shall see in the next chapter, that many competitors are imitating this way to organize the business, and that most of them are achieving success.

Subcontracting in the automobile industry revisited: the Japanese way

The kind of organization set up by Benetton is not only successful in the low margin textile business. We saw in Chapter 4 how the mechanisms that the Western automobile manufacturers set up to make sure their subcontractors did not run away with too large a fraction of the value generated by the system were intrinsically inefficient. But, if told so, they would have surely answered that there was no other way to lower costs and protect their margins. That this almost confrontational way to manage such an important relationship was the only viable one had truly become the industry's common wisdom.

But Japanese manufacturers did not partake in that wisdom. For a number a reasons, both cultural and economic, they set up a completely different system, one that has many of the characteristics of the Benetton network.[3]

The first important difference between Japanese and Western manufacturers is the sheer extent of subcontracting. In the late 1980s Toyota produced roughly 4.5 million cars per year with 65,000 employees, or 70 cars per employee. It took General Motors 750,000 to produce 8 million cars, or 10 cars per employee. Most of the difference is *not* due to a difference in productivity, but to Toyota's practice of outsourcing practically everything needed to assemble the car. In general, for a company of comparable size, the Japanese subcontract up to twice as many parts as Western companies do. Thus the Japanese companies are more de-integrated to start with. But the real difference is, as mentioned above, their relationship with their subcontractors. As we shall see now, the whole method is radically different.

Let us take the case of Toyota, the company that 'invented' some of the key features of the system. Instead of having an arm's-length relationship with a number of suppliers, each of which gets to do only piecemeal work, Toyota relies on a veritable network of more than 150 'primary' subcontractors. These subcontractors specialize in complete sub-systems, such as seats, brakes, or ignition kits. They are regular providers, i.e. the subcontractor on seats knows that, barring exceptional circumstances, it will deliver the seats of each new model. In fact Toyota expects it to design the seat, working from a set of target specifications: dimensions, quality, characteristics, final cost. The supplier works from there, applying all its accumulated expertise in seat-making, to design a seat that will conform to specifications. Price is not arrived at through a bidding process, for there are usually only one or two subcontractors who can do the job anyway. Price is arrived at through the study of everybody's costs, and the application of a 'reasonable' mark up.

Once the job is specified, the primary contractor turns to a tier of 'secondary' subcontractors (more than 5000 for the whole Toyota system) that deliver most of the parts necessary to assemble the seat. Again, the relationship between primary and secondary subcontractors is a stable one: each primary subcontractor has its network of secondary subcontractors to which they turn on a regular basis for their inputs. There are financial links underpinning the relationships: Toyota owns minority stakes in many primary subcontractors, and those own minority stakes in many secondary subcontractors. Finally, there is a large number of companies (up to 40,000) that lie more at the periphery of the system: they deliver only on a non-continuous basis, or are in turn subcontracted to second-tier companies.

In this system there is relatively little intra-system competition: each primary subcontractor specializes in one area, which is its domain. It is not constantly being threatened with losing its business to another subcontractor. That will happen only if quality or costs get really out of hand. But even then Toyota will not 'drop' the subcontractor. It will rather shift a higher proportion of its orders to the other subcontractor specializing in the same area, and start working with the subcontractor in trouble to find out what its problems are, and help fix them.

In effect the superiority of this networking system over the traditional Western arm's-length approach is clear when we look at it in dynamic terms. Under the typical Western relationship there is very little learning. Subcontractors cannot contribute anything to the sub-system for which they are working, for they only deliver isolated parts, devoid of any working context. Thus all the design quality must come from the car manufacturer, who implicitly despises all the input that could come from hundreds of companies that are, after all, specialist engineering firms.

Second, any advance in manufacturing methods that may occur is kept carefully hidden from the rest of the system. If a typical Western subcontractor ever finds a way to improve its manufacturing skills, thus increasing quality and/or decreasing costs, it has every reason not to let anybody know about it. If the car manufacturer finds out, it will adjust the prices down accordingly; if other subcontractors find out, they will become fiercer competitors. Thus any learning that takes place does not spread beyond the specific company, and has few results for the competitiveness of the final car being offered to the customer.

In the Toyota system all subcontractors have a clear sense of working 'on the same side', i.e. on Toyota's. Their future depends very clearly on Toyota's success; and they will work for it. If anybody finds a 'better way', it is in their interest to make sure that all subcontractors in the network adopt it, for this will make the final product more competitive, thus ensuring future sales and profits for the whole network. In Toyota's system competition happens at the 'network level', not at the individual company level: it is a competition of Toyota's network against Nissan's network, not of Toyota against its suppliers. Note that this does not make the industry any less competitive. If at all, competition is fiercer. But it is displaced to the final market place, not to the relations between companies that need each other.

In fact group feeling is very strong within those networks, probably stronger that within many vertically integrated Western companies. Japanese manufacturers have supplier associations that hold yearly meetings to share knowledge and improvements. Those associations have been used to spread very quickly crucial manufacturing techniques, such as statistical process control, total quality control, value engineering, computer-aided design, etc. If all the small, incremental learning that takes place in a network of several thousand companies is somehow disseminated throughout, the cumulative effect over the years will be devastating to competitors.

Thus the Japanese system helps car manufacturers in all the steps of the process. First, it helps them 'design for manufacture', i.e. make sure the designs are easy to manufacture in an efficient, high-quality way. Evidently, the only real way to design for manufacture is to let the eventual manufacturer into the design process very early. That is what the Japanese system encourages, and the traditional Western one impedes. In Japan subcontractors are a valued, experienced part of the team, whose opinion is critical. In the West subcontractors are almost 'the enemy', to be kept as far away as possible from the source of real profits, i.e. knowledge.

The Japanese method also helps the manufacturing process itself, as we have seen, by encouraging system-wide transfer of learning. This, together with the specialization encouraged by the system (again impossible in the Western approach), helps drive costs down. As the learning curve takes effect, prices are brought down in a way that lets the subcontractor keep part of the increased margins, for there is clear agreement up-front on how the extra profits generated by learning and innovation will be shared between the subcontractor and the car manufacturer.

Finally, the system is essential when it comes to some of the critical cost reduction techniques, such as just-in-time inventory management. Such a technique demands complete trust and cooperation between the supplier and the assembler. Without them, all that happens is that inventory gets pushed from the assembler to the subcontractor, who has to keep it 'just in case'. Then there are no savings, just one more case of the car assembler trying to push down the supplier's margins.

The result of course is well known: Japanese cars that, when they reach the final customer, are of such better quality and can be sold profitably at a such a lower price that, without political protection, the Japanese would have all but destroyed the Western companies. The way the car manufacturers deal with the subcontractors is not the only explanation for that success, but, as I have shown here, *it is at the core of some of the most important aspects*: continuous quality improvement, continuous cost reduction, extremely 'lean' manufacturing, smooth flow of materials and components, design for manufacture, etc. Once again, as in the case of Benetton, we find that the company can do something that is strategically very valuable only because of its sophisticated networking arrangements. Fully integrated companies could not deliver, but arm's length relationships, of the sort described in the previous chapter cannot either. It takes this mixture of long-term, 'solid' relationships, individual entrepreneurship and flexibility that we have called a strategic network to give dynamic competitive advantages.

As in the case of Benetton, the superiority of the system is shown by the fact that it is being adopted by most competitors ... successfully. Thus there is nothing intrinsically Japanese about the arrangement, although specific Japanese culture and circumstances may have played a role in its discovery. But the system itself is transferable, as proved by the ability of several Western manufacturers, which have made impressive progress trying to set up their own network, to adopt 'lean manufacturing' techniques.

The system is not unique to car making. In fact the famous Japanese *keiretsu* have most of the characteristics of a strategic network: a hub company, investments (financial and otherwise) in long-term relationships, and a policy of specialization within the network. When a company within a *keiretsu* does not perform, the hub company (normally one of the huge trading houses such as Mitsui or Mitsubishi, or a large bank) sends executives to solve its problems. Stability is not sought, as in the West, by having many sources of inputs and many different clients, so as not to be dependent on anyone, but on long-term relationships and the implicit pact that problems will be sorted out in a fair way.

Strategic networks afford companies the chance to make the necessary long-term investments in specific relationships, ones that cannot be justified in arm's length subcontracting relationships, but maintain high flexibility and entrepreneurial drive (which get zapped relatively easily in a vertically integrated company). In fact they push competition towards the 'tip' of the whole business system (where it meets the final consumer), insisting on cooperation inside it. Thus, traditionally, General Motors has competed with Ford *and* with its subcontractors, while Toyota has 'only' competed with the other car manufacturers. This is, in essence, what happens within a company: although there may be some rivalry for promotions, all employees are supposed to cooperate in order to achieve the profitability of the company, thus indirectly ensuring their own success. This is not very different from the approach that a subcontractor within a strategic network takes. But the advantages of subcontracting, against vertical integration, which we saw in the previous chapter, are not lost: 'fat' is not accumulated, flexibility is maintained, entrepreneurship and innovation flourish.

Working from the two examples we have just seen, and adding new ones, the next chapter will try to derive a general framework for strategic networks – what is really their essence, what gives them their unusual combination of stability and flexibility, in what industries are they most appropriate, and how can they be set up and maintained.

References

1 This description of the company draws heavily on earlier materials, particularly J.C. Jarillo and J.I. Martínez, 'Benetton S.p.A.', Harvard Business School case, 1988; and J.C. Jarillo and H.H. Stevenson, 'Co-operative strategies: the payoffs and the pitfalls', *Long Range Planning*, vol. 24, No. 1, 1991.
2 'Profiles-Being everywhere', *New Yorker*, 10 November 1986, pp. 53–74.
3 See James P. Womack, Daniel T. Jones and Daniel Roos, *The Machine That Changed The World*, New York: Rawson Associates, 1990; also Clark, Kim and Takahiro Fujimoto, *Product Development Performance*, Boston: Harvard Business School Press, 1991.

Part Three How to Set Up
and Manage a Strategtic Network

6 The essence of a strategic network

We try in this chapter to portray what is the essence of a strategic network. Deepening our inquiry, from a few examples to a general framework, is absolutely necessary if valid conclusions are to be drawn for other contexts.[1]

Understanding a strategic network is not easy. In spite of the detailed examples just presented, I'm convinced that many a reader will still be thinking that the 'trick' is to set up a system where the 'hub' company simply 'controls' the rest. After all, what would Benetton subcontractors be without Benetton? They are completely at the large company's mercy, ready to be dumped when its interests so demand. Something similar could be said of the Japanese networks, where perks such as life-time employment only really accrue to employees of the large company in the centre, not to the constellation of smaller firms around it.

This 'sceptical' look at inter-company cooperation is perfectly understandable. We have been reared in a context where it is taken for granted that the world of business is one of 'everybody for himself'. In this sense it is interesting to note that all the first writings on networks as forms of coordinating stable relationships among different organizations were produced by sociologists working outside the field of business. The networks they described had to do with universities, health-care centres, and other non-profit-making institutions. Business writers did not find it a useful concept for many years.

This neglect was probably aggravated by the pre-eminence of the school of 'competitive advantage' in the past few years. That mode of thinking, best represented by the work of

Michael Porter, essentially affirms that the profits that a company can expect to make are determined, first by the profit potential of its industry, and second by its position within it. And the profit potential of the industry is dependent on how easy it is to get in, how intense rivalry among existing competitors is, and how easy it is for suppliers and customers to capture the value being created by the industry. Thus, in order to prosper, a company has to compete not only with its current competitors but also with all potential ones, with its suppliers and with its clients.[2] As we have seen, this 'atomistic' view of economic activity, in which each player is alone against the world, may not be the most efficient way to compete.

But this does not deny the obvious fact that companies are out there to make money. Thus we need a framework where we can reconcile what seems to be the essence of economic activity in a market economy, i.e. competition, and what seems to be at the core of many successes, i.e. cooperation.

Competition and cooperation

R.H. Coase, Nobel prize winner in 1991, was the first economist to become interested in the issue of why companies organize some activities inside, i.e. through vertical integration, while other activities are left to outsiders. In a seminal 1937 article[3] he concluded, along the lines we have been following in this book, that there are essentially two ways to organize economic activity – within companies and in open markets.

The essence of a company is cooperation. People join companies because they obtain a satisfactory return for their work; and that return is generated because of the joint work of all the people in the company. The essence of a company, looking inwards, is cooperation. Without it, there would be no point in joining. In fact in those activities where people do not need the cooperation of other people to perform, there are no companies; from opera singers to independent insurance agents, if the goal can be achieved individually (or with very few people) companies do not arise. When the goal requires the coordinated effort of many people, probably backed by important capital investments, we see traditional companies dominate the field.

Those companies compete then with each other. As we saw in Chapter 2, the essence of sustainable profitability for any given economic activity is that it can be performed in a unique way, i.e. that the company performing it cannot be replaced by another company that can do the same thing, at the same cost, and may be ready to take a slightly lower margin. As cooperation is the essence of intra-company relationships, competition seems to be the essence of inter-company relationships.

The difference between cooperation and competition can be put as the difference between a zero-sum game and a non-zero-sum game. Poker is a zero-sum game: the amount made by the winners is exactly equal to the amount lost by the losers. In monetary terms there cannot be a 'net gain' out of a poker table. That is an intrinsically competitive situation: one player's gain depends on somebody's loss. If I get the order, you lose; if I charge you £1 more, you will make £1 less.

In a non-zero-sum game there can be a net gain (or a net loss). A game may be set up so that, if a particular result occurs, both players make money. Evidently, in a true game situation, that money must come from somewhere. But it need not be somebody's loss, it may be the money spectators are prepared to pay to enjoy watching the game. In that situation nobody loses: all the players get money from people who do not lose it, but are willingly exchanging it for some entertainment.

In economic terms one can approach a relationship as a zero-sum game or not. For instance, a specific negotiation between a company and its trade union can be seen as a zero-sum game: the extra money the workers get will come straight out of the company's profits. But it can also be viewed as a non-zero sum game: if the company and the unions reach a prompt, efficient agreement, with some sort of profit-sharing mechanisms, *both* the company and the union can make more money than if they go on arguing. They can also, through a prolonged strike, both lose money. Seen like this, it is certainly a non-zero-sum game. In the first case the competitive view prevails. The second takes into account the opportunity for cooperation.

It is not difficult to extend the argument to the relation between a company and one of its suppliers (or customers). When negotiating a price, it may seem that they are engaged in a zero-sum game, and that is indeed the typical competitive view. But they can also realize that, by cooperating, the may increase the total pie to be shared, thus turning the game into a non-zero-sum one.

Thus the identification of cooperation with intra-company behaviour and competition with inter-company relationships depends on how one defines the boundaries of the 'company', i.e. the area within which cooperation reigns and outside which competition is paramount; for, as we have seen in the examples of the previous chapter, the boundary between cooperation and competition does not have to coincide necessarily with the legal boundaries of a firm. There can be cooperation across companies, and competition within them.

In fact we are talking here about two dimensions that cross each other: whether two units cooperate or compete, and whether those two units have common ownership or not. The implicit assumption in the difficulty of understanding inter-company cooperation is that most people automatically identify common ownership with cooperation, and non-common ownership with competition. But we can show in Figure 6.1 how these two dimensions interact.

The top row shows that a company may or may not in fact be based on cooperation. In the first case we find a company with a strong sense of shared goals, a clear understanding that 'we are all in this together'. The approach is a cooperative one, and all the players belong to the same owner. In the second case, even with a common owner, there is no such goal congruence: each unit plays its own game, in an adversarial relationship with the others. It is one of the characteristics of bureaucracies.

	Cooperative approach	Non-cooperative approach
Common ownership	Vertically integrated company	Bureaucracy
No common ownership	Strategic network	Market

Figure 6.1 *Interactions between ownership mode and approach to the relationship*

The bottom row shows, on the right-hand side, a typical arm's-length market relationship, where independent units compete with each other. But the other box shows the relationship that underlies a strategic network: a situation where independent units consider their relationship a cooperative one, because they believe there will be more to share (and it will be shared fairly) by cooperating. This kind of relationship has many of the characteristics of a 'hierarchical' relationship: relatively unstructured tasks, 'open-ended' contracts, implicit assumption of stable relationships, etc. But it is maintained between companies that are, *de jure* and *de facto*, independent units.[4] But their motivation to join, and to stay in, the network are the same as those of a worker joining a company: the belief that by working with others he or she will be more productive, and (at least part of) that productivity will be passed down to him or her.

When is cooperation the most appropriate way?

We have explained so far what a strategic network is. The task is now to understand how it can be more efficient than any other mode of organization. Going back to Coase's question, we ask not only when an activity is integrated vertically or contracted in the market, but when it would be most efficiently coordinated within a strategic network.

As we have seen in detail in the case of Benetton, some activities are most efficiently carried out outside the hub firm, while others are most efficiently carried out inside. Thus, in a first analysis, the decision is quite simple: the activity will be internalized if the internal cost (IC) of doing it is lower than the price charged by an external supplier (EP). This, as we saw in Chapter 3 is not uncommon, particularly if we take a long-term view. But if that were simply the case, there would be no vertical integration, for companies that integrated would pay a heavy penalty. The reason we do find vertical integration, even in cases where an outside supplier could be more efficient, is that the company has to add the cost of the transaction to the supplier's external price. Thus the true cost of doing things outside (external cost, EC) is the external price plus the transaction cost: $EC = EP + TC$. An activity will then be integrated efficiently only if $EP + TC > IC$, i.e. if the sum of the price charged by the supplier plus the transaction cost is higher than the internal cost.

The intriguing point is that this may happen even if the external price charged by the supplier is lower than the cost of doing things internally, i.e. if $IC > EP$. Going back to the automobile industry, we saw how having whole sub-sub-subsystems delivered by specialized suppliers was in itself cheaper than doing the detailed design and consolidation of the different parts in-house. But Western manufacturers did not go external with that design and consolidation because they feared that, by so doing, the suppliers would eventually start capturing too high a proportion of the value, for they would become the real experts in say, brakes. That fear of a future erosion in profits is a clear example of a transaction cost. It would be cheaper in a 'theoretical world' to subcontract the activity, but in this real, competitive world, the company plays safe and integrates the activity. Thus even if IC > EP, the presence of TC forces integration.

Those transaction costs depend very much on the nature of the activity itself. Clearly some circumstances are more 'difficult' than others. The reader may remember the example, used in Chapter 3, of the rolling of hot steel: rolling steel is done by the same company that makes the steel, because by rolling it as it comes out the blast furnace, the rolling operation does not have to reheat the steel, thus saving energy costs, and making the integrated company more efficient. But this, although it is a textbook example of a case where vertical integration is more efficient, does not prove that vertical integration is more efficient, it simply proves that steel has to be rolled as it comes out of the furnace. There is no economic reason why the owner of the furnace and the owner of the rolling mill must be the same.

Or is there? What could happen if the two activities were performed by different companies? Certainly they would be critically dependent on each other. Imagine that, once the rolling mill has been built, the steel maker decides to ask for a higher price for its steel. What could the roller do? Not much, but pay. It could of course have set up a complex contract, trying to foresee every possible contingency, and be prepared to enforce it by law. But if the costs of lawyers are added up, together with the costs of dreaming up the contracts, of trying to protect oneself from possible 'tricks', the real costs go up so much that the transaction is not feasible. But since there is an economic gain to be made by rolling the steel hot out of the furnace, the standard solution is for the company to integrate both activities: no contracts, no lawyers, no problems, because no (market) transaction.

This is, in the end, the rationale for much vertical integration of activities that could be carried out more efficiently outside: the nature of the transaction involves specific assets, or puts the players in such an 'awkward' position, that it is really better to do things inside. After all, we saw how Benetton did not subcontract dyeing, partially for these reasons. Thus, in the presence of high transaction costs, companies will integrate activities that could have been subcontracted, i.e. whose external price is lower than the internal cost, thus paying an unavoidable efficiency penalty.

But let us assume for a second that a particular company is able somehow to lower those transaction costs. Then it would pay to subcontract. As a result, the company would be less integrated than its competitors and more efficient, for it would capture the efficiency of doing things outside without paying the penalty of the transaction cost. This is the essence of a strategic network: a company finds a way to lower transaction costs, which, until then, were forcing competitors to integrate. By so doing, it gains efficiency over its competitors, and sets up a system that, as we saw in the previous chapter is also more flexible, for it has the advantages of independent units.

The condition for the economic efficiency of a strategic network is, then, that the external price be lower than the internal cost for some important activities, *and* that transactions costs be lowered, so as to make the transaction economic. If transaction costs are generally low to start with, there is no network; there is a simple market relationship where everybody subcontracts (few companies would think of integrating their office supplies, for instance). If transactions costs are high, and not lowered, there is vertical integration. Only if they are lowered by a specific company does the network arise. The three cases are shown below:

EP < IC, TC generally low: market relationship
EP < IC, TC generally high: vertical integration
                             (inefficiency absorbed)
EP < IC, TC selectively low: strategic network

How to reduce transactions costs

As we saw above, transaction costs stem from the difficulty of perfectly predicting everything that will happen in the future. Oliver Williamson, who first dealt with transaction costs in detail,[5] gives, as the key reasons for transaction costs to arise, the following four factors: our inability to analyse everything in advance (which he calls, following Nobel prize-winner

Herbert Simon, 'man's bounded rationality');[6] the fact that in business the future is always uncertain; the presence of few players for a given kind of transaction, i.e. few suppliers or few buyers of the product or service in question; and the possibility that some of the players be 'opportunistic', i.e. try to take advantage of the others.

If we think about real-life situations, we will see that it is really the last point about opportunism that is worrying, but it gets amplified by the previous ones. Thus we don't really fear opportunistic behaviour if there is no scarcity of suppliers, so we can always go to a different one, or if the transaction can be very clearly specified in advance, etc. It is really the possibility that we can be 'taken' that constitutes the problem of the transaction costs; and that fear, that mistrust, is particularly appropriate when one player invests in a specialization that is only useful when working for the other, which is one of the characteristics of strategic networks, as we have seen. Being able to generate trust, then, is the key to reducing transactions costs, thus making the existence of a strategic network economically feasible.

H.B. Thorelli, one of the first business writers on networks, has defined trust as 'an assumption or reliance on the part of A that if either A or B encounters a problem in the fulfillment of his implicit or explicit transactional obligations, B may be counted on to do what A would do if B's resources were at A's disposal'.[7] Observe that trust dissolves the need to specify unforeseeable consequences, for it is assumed that the decision rule to be followed by A will be identical to the decision rule to be followed by B. The same can be said of the problem of 'fair sharing' of future, unspecified profits that should accrue through cooperation. When there is trust, the need of pre-specifying every possible future outcome and of setting up mechanisms to prevent or correct opportunistic behaviour is greatly diminished.

Generating trust

How can trust be generated? Let us take the situation of the business person who needs to generate trust in order to build a network, i.e. in order to lower transaction costs arising from opportunism and asset-specificity. He or she will have to act on two variables: the assumptions of the owner of the resource (the other party) regarding the entrepreneur's motivation, and the intrinsic situation.

The first variable can be addressed through choosing the partners to the different relationships carefully, searching explicitly for people the entrepreneur can relate to, i.e. with similar values. This identity of values and motivations will certainly facilitate the emergence of trust.

The second variable is the intrinsic situation. The entrepreneur cannot expect 'blind trust' if it means the members of the network must put themselves at high risk. Trusting behaviour can only be generated by showing that the entrepreneur would be worse off if he or she behaved opportunistically. This is what economists colourfully call 'interchanging hostages'. In medieval times an efficient way to make sure that a given treaty between two kings would be honoured was by interchanging their respective sons or daughters. If the pact was not respected, they were put to death. Benetton could certainly take advantage of one of their smaller subcontractors but what would the effect be on the system as a whole? Is the gain to be had by hurting one of the subcontractors worth the loss of efficiency that would come from the deterioration of the system? Obviously not, and that is why the situation is, even for the smaller subcontractors, much less risky than it seems. Opportunistic behaviour quickly destroys reputation, and reputation has a huge economic value when setting up relationships, for it sustains trust, as we have seen.[8] Thus a company which has set up a system based on its good reputation cannot act against it. Its reputation is the 'hostage' it has given to its partners.

This is how trust is *maintained*. But how can it be *developed* in the first place? The critical component is to have a long-term approach to the relationship, because it makes it clear that the relationship is itself is considered valuable. Therefore opportunistic behaviour which would cause a severance of the relationship, will be considered less likely.

A well-known problem in game theory is the prisoner's

dilemma, which we will use as a starting point in our analysis. Take the case of two burglars, Peter and Paul, who have been caught by the police. The police has only very thin evidence, so they want them to confess. The burglars are kept separate, and each is told that if he confesses, he will be set free. But, based on his confession, the other will get a ten-year sentence. If neither talks, they get a two-year sentence each. If both talk, they both get five years. Under these circumstances, it makes sense for both prisoners to talk, i.e. not to cooperate with each other, even if they know they would be better off cooperating. This is because cooperating (not talking) would put each of them at an unbearable risk: if Peter shuts up and Paul talks, Peter gets 'rewarded' with the worst possible outcome, while Paul gets free. Since both must presume the other is in the same situation, the only rational behaviour is not to cooperate with each other, i.e. to confess and get a five-year sentence as a 'lesser evil'. Figure 6.2 summarizes the situation.

Peter talks Paul talks Peter: 5 years Paul: 5 years	Peter does not talk Paul talks Peter: 10 years Paul: goes free
Peter talks Paul does not talk Peter: goes free Paul: 10 years	Peter does not talk Paul does not talk Peter: 2 years Paul: 2 years

Figure 6.2 *Different outcomes for the players caught in the prisoner's dilemma*

This situation, which is very common, can be generalized as follows. T is the best possible payoff, achieved through cheating (getting free, in our example); R is what happens to both players if both of them cooperate; P is what happens to both players if they do not cooperate; finally, S (the 'sucker's payoff') is the worst possible outcome and happens to the player that is cheated, i.e. collaborates while the other does not. The generalized form of the problem is $T > R > P > S$, and $(T + S) < 2*R$.

With these relations, as shown in the example, it is better for each player not to cooperate regardless of what the other player does. In game theory jargon, not to cooperate is a 'dominant strategy' for both players, so that the expected outcome of the game is not to cooperate for both players, resulting in the payoff pair P,P. Since this outcome is worse than the cooperative outcome R,R, the result is highly negative.

In our context, given that many situations that arise in a business relationship can be represented in this way, we encounter great difficulty in sustaining networks. An example is joint R&D. If several firms decide to take on a given project in a cooperative way, it is to the best advantage of each of them to send a second-class scientist to the project, while expecting that the others will send their best. No firm wants to send its best, fearing that the others will send their seconds and get a free ride. So everybody sends seconds, and the project fails.

The prisoner's dilemma is a good formalization of the basic problem of lack of trust. In spite of the obvious benefit of cooperation (the prisoner's dilemma is an excellent example of a non-zero sum game!), there is a strong temptation to default and take a larger benefit. But, even more important, our own fears of being fooled (thus getting the 'sucker's payoff') induce us to act first and not cooperate. Since both parties, in a rational way, should think along the same lines (and both know it), we end up at the inefficient point, i.e. the relationship is not possible.

How can a business person confront such a negative situation? A first obvious direction will be to try to change the game being played, i.e. the relationships among the different payoffs, or the payoffs themselves. Any effort in this direction is worthwhile and can help one to avoid the dilemma by eliminating it. But it is not always easy to change the game so that the temptation is avoided. One trivial way to do it is for the two players to sign a contract or agreement, so that both players are committed to cooperate. But contracts are often not enforceable, at least at a reasonable cost: this is precisely the essence of transaction costs, as we have seen. The problem is even worse than it seems. Games theory tells us that, even if we repeat this game any finite number of times, by backward induction we can easily see that no cooperation for both is the only equilibrium for this game.

Intuition, however, strongly suggests that repetition should foster cooperation, in spite of theoretical assertions. An experiment sheds light on the value of repetition. In his book, *The Evolution of Cooperation* Robert Axelrod describes a computer game with characteristics similar to those of the prisoner's dilemma.[9] Many professional game theorists were ready to play the role of one of the players and submitted computer subroutines to be pitted against all other submitted routines. The game was repeated 200 times, and everybody knew that was to be the case. This was an 'empirical way' of testing which strategy was actually better, one of cooperation or one of competition. The winner was a very simple routine submitted by Professor Anatol Rapoport from the University of Toronto. His strategy is now known as 'tit-for-tat'.

The strategy specifies the following rule: start by cooperating, and at any other stage do exactly what your opponent did in the previous move. That's all. This strategy proved to be robust even against players that knew that this strategy was the winner in the first round. Furthermore, it also stood up to some evolutive simulation where the winning strategies reproduced themselves and changed the environment for the next round. Therefore there seems to be hope that cooperation can survive and end up dominating even in a world of mistrust and non-cooperation.

In analysing the traits of the winning strategy, Axelrod finds three relevant characteristics: first, the strategy is 'nice', since it never starts a non-cooperative move by itself; second, it is 'provocable', i.e. it gets mad at defectors quickly and retaliates; third, it is 'forgiving', since retaliation is only proportional to the length of defection. These three good personality traits of being nice, provocable, and forgiving, seem to be the essence of both the robustness of the strategy and its survival in an aggressive environment.

Without trying to push the analogy too far, we may think that these are personality traits we should find in an entrepreneur able to create and sustain a network. It also gives us hope that cooperation can survive even in a non-cooperative environment and end up being the prevalent way of doing business. Note that the robustness of the strategy indicates that it is beneficial to have a reputation for being a tit-for-tat, since it beats more aggressive behaviour in the long run, even if designed against it. Finally, note that this strategy never really beats its opponent; at most they end up equal. The benefit comes, first, from doing well on average against any opponent, and, second, from taking a non-zero-sum approach, i.e. this strategy may not ensure the biggest share of a pie, but it does ensure a good share of the biggest pie.

This shows, in an experimental way that closely ressembles day-to-day business experience, that taking a long-term approach *does* change the outcome, and may be at the basis of a winning strategy. Let us then try to incorporate this insight into our basic prisoner's dilemma.

To be more realistic, the game has to include an uncertainty factor, p. This means that the game will be repeated with probability p, depending (presumably) upon the satisfactory results of previous games, among other things. Then the probability that the relationship will still survive in period T is p^t, that is, if the chances of getting to play a new game are of 90 per cent (probability of 0.9), then the chances of playing two games are 0.9^2. In this environment the incentive to cheat in a particular game, thus interrupting the game for sure, is tempered by the loss of future potential gains, for it is a non-zero-sum game. Being nice is the entry ticket to a potential future, profitable game.

Obviously the results of the game depend on the value of p

– on how much one believes that good behaviour does indeed open possibilities for future profits. It can be seen that, as p increases, so does the incentive for cooperation. Following the case in Figure 6.2, the incentive for not cooperating is $T - R$. But if cooperation is lost forever, we must take into account the $R - P$ loss that comes from it, adjusted by the probability of having more chances to play. In other words, the opportunistic gain is sure, while the future loss depends on the probability of having more games to play. We can calculate a value for p that corresponds to the cut-off point between cooperation and non-cooperation. Thus, the future value of cooperation is

$$p \, \frac{(R - P)}{1 - p}$$

Therefore, there will be cooperation if

$$T - R > p \, \frac{(R - P)}{1 - p}$$

The cut-off value can be found by solving $(T - R)(1 - p) = p(R - P)$.

The result is $p = (T - R)/(T - P)$. If the parties think that there is at least a chance of p for long-term repetition of the game, they will cooperate.

Given our interpretation of the game as a strategic network relationship between two parties, it seems that an infinite game with discounting that incorporates a probability of continuation is an acceptable representation of the situation. We are, in essence, saying that the threat of severing the relationship becomes the main deterrent to non cooperation, provided the threat is credible. In other words, people will not cheat if they want to go on doing business in the future.

The lesson to be obtained from these results is that cooperation can be developed, even allowing for opportunistic behaviour. There are three points to remember :

1 Repetition permits cooperation, and hence the importance of a long-term outlook.
2 Threats must be credible.
3 The discount factor matters. The impatience in the agreement makes it more difficult. Also interesting is that p can be lowered and the cooperation equilibrium still hold if we include the possibility of penalties.

It is not difficult to see how these points apply to real networks, such as Benetton's or Toyota's. The long-term outlook is always present, expected behaviour clear, and punishments handed down, when necessary, in a 'fair' way.

Thus both the theoretical solutions and the empirical analysis show the same characteristics in the optimal strategy to foster cooperation. In summary, be nice, provocable and forgiving, always stressing the future gains to be had from present cooperation, to de-emphasize hard bargaining over current deals. Furthermore, any particular situation can be represented as a game like the one in our example. If we are able to modify the game, we can make cooperation somewhat easier. We can try to reduce the temptation level, we can include stronger punishments and make them cheap to implement, or we can try to modify the discount factor by increasing the (perceived) probability of continuing the relationship. Building a reputation becomes essential, for it clearly introduces the long-term factor.

Trust is essential. This is not surprising, for we have seen that it is at the root of cooperation. Two general avenues can be used to create cooperation:

1 Develop long-term relationships.
2 Try to modify the game, acting upon the four variables (cooperation reward, opportunistic gain, punishment, sucker's payoff) and keeping in mind the importance of the future.

The network's internal consistency

We have seen in the first part of this chapter how a strategic network can be more efficient, in general terms, than any other way to coordinate economic activities. But this is not enough. A network has also to be effective, in the sense that makes it attractive to all participants to stay in it; for, as we have been repeating, it is essential to a network that its players are committed to investment in it. Without that specialized investment, a network is no more than a collection of suppliers and buyers, but there is no special competitive advantage being gained by the network itself. But that gain has to be shared in a way that all participants feel to be fair. This is what I call the effectiveness of a network. Thus, in order to prosper, a network has to be both efficient and effective: it has to beat other organizational forms, and it has to distribute the gains in a way that fosters loyalty, for without this loyalty there is no network, and no gains.

It is the specialized investments that give 'consistency' to the network. It is the knowledge that Toyota's suppliers have of Toyota's way; even the machines they buy just to serve Toyota better can glue the network together. For the network really to function it has to have more consistency inside than with its environment, the relationships within it have to be clearly 'denser' and deeper than without. Once again, the examples we saw help illustrate this point: the better adapted to each other's working ways the members of a network become, through cooperation and specialized investments, the more efficient coordination becomes, thus paving the way for more and more adaptation. (This also increases risk but we will come back to this point.)

Thus the whole system is self-reinforcing, for every characteristic of the network builds on the others: adaptation, specialization, trust, long-term outlook, internal consistency *vis-à-vis* the outside world, etc., which provide efficiency and flexibility. Those deliver a good competitive position, justifying the existence of the network and reinforcing its characteristics.

But networks are not, obviously, the only game in town. After seeing what a network is, and what the conditions for its existence are, let us turn now to the basic question of what are the circumstances where a network makes most sense, for, as any other organizational form, a network's comparative efficiency depends on the task at hand. There is no such things as the 'best' organizational arrangement, just solutions more or less attuned to solving specific problems.

When is a strategic network the appropriate response?

The first characteristic that a business system has to have to make it amenable to a networking solution is that some of its critical activities have advantages if carried out in a de-integrated way. We saw in Chapters 3 and 4 what the reasons for that may be.

- First, widely differing optimal scales, i.e. that the optimal way to perform some activities be through very large companies, while some other activities be best carried out by small ones.
- Second, some activities may require a very specific 'culture' or mentality within the company. If the relevant mentalities vary widely across the different activities in the business system, a de-integrated relationship will probably be more efficient than trying to keep them in-house and then creating more or less artificial barriers between them.
- Third, the business is such that innovation comes mostly through the entrepreneurial motivation of relatively small units. This is the case in Benetton, where we saw how gains in efficiency do not come from important R&D projects, but from a host of small improvements; or in Toyota's impressive manufacturing system, where accumulated learning also comes from small, incremental improvements.
- Fourth, the different activities that make up the business system can expect, from a structural point of view, widely different rates of profitability, because barriers to entry and competitive advantages apply to them in widely different degrees.

But these are general reasons to de-integrate and, as such, they could recommend that the business system be coordinated through a collection of arm's-length market relationships. To make the network solution advisable, there has to be a need for coordination exceeding that which is available through simple subcontracting.

Thus whenever specific investments, be it in machinery, know-how or, more generally, ways of doing business, would result in higher efficiency, but most of the above conditions prevail, then a networking solution makes sense. Equally, when speed is important, to react faster and faster to market and competitive realities, leaving coordination to arm's-length market mechanisms can be inefficient or inflexible. If innovation demands understanding of the whole system, then again a networking relationship seems appropriate. Whenever close coordination of the whole business system is required but vertical integration would be inefficient, then a strategic network may be the best response.

We have seen throughout this book several examples of industries that have those characteristics, from apparel to fast food, from cars to computers. But if we look at the essence of what a network is, we realize that its characteristics sound attractive for many more industries. The reason this form of organization is still spreading is that it takes a creative manager to adapt the formula to the very different realities (technological, competitive) of each industry. But once that is done, as we saw, it is quickly copied by the rest. More than twenty years passed between the appearance of strategic networks in fast food and the emergence of the Benetton system. But very few years lapsed between the imitation by their competitors of McDonald's and Benetton's. The current strong move towards de-integration in most industries will have to be tempered by networking; many companies are already discovering that transaction costs do exist, and that coordinating outsiders is not as inexpensive as it first seems.

Setting up and managing (in) a strategic network

From what we have been saying all along, it should now be clear that to set up a network requires, first, that the network make sense economically, i.e. that it be an efficient way of coordinating the specific business system at hand; and second, that the person or company starting it be able to lower transaction costs by developing trust.

By definition, trust cannot be imposed. It has to be earned. Thus developing trust will probably imply a long-term process, where the originator of the network develops, little by little, personal relationships and a reputation for fairness.

In this sense it is not surprising that many networks have a strong geographical or cultural component. By setting up business relationships with people the entrepreneur already knows, he or she can play on a pre-existing track record of personal integrity. The difficulty that many Japanese companies are having when trying to set similar networks to theirs in the West resides, at least partially, in the mistrust with which most people approach somebody whose culture, both general and business, is greatly different. Conversely, the success in business of many ethnic groups, be it emigrant Chinese in South East Asia or orthodox Jews in the diamond trade, stems probably from the low transaction costs to be found among member of those groups, who can trust each other because there is already a strong tradition of honesty – and a clear possibility of 'social punishment' if business is not conducted in all fairness.

But even more important is how the hub company manages its relationships with the other members of the network. In a way it is not very different than the hierarchical relationship within a company, as we have seen.

It has been said that subcontracting practices are simply a mechanism by which large companies would export some of their risk in business to smaller, defenseless subcontractors. The larger companies would, for instance, keep production in-house when demand was slack, thus avoiding layoffs. The relationship would then be based on 'exporting' all the risk to the subcontractors. That would certainly go against the trust-building practices that we should expect in efficient networks. Thus we should expect the hub company to take on some of the risk of the relationship, through an agreement that shifts (at least) part of the random variance in the subcontractor's costs to the large company. In other words, there should be a factor α that represents the share of risk taken up by the large company. Thus if $\alpha = 0$, then the subcontractor bears all the risk (it is a purely fixed-price contract); if $\alpha = 1$, the large company bears all the risk (it is a cost-plus contract).

The problem with $\alpha = 0$ is that there is no real network relationship (it would be the case of buying something at a given, fixed price, with no further connection between the firms). The problem with $\alpha = 1$ is that there is no incentive whatsoever for the subcontractor to be efficient. Efficient networks therefore should show a factor α that is larger than 0 but smaller than 1. There is some evidence of this. Kawasaki and McMillan examined a large sample of subcontracting arrangements among Japanese firms and found that many of those arrangements have the hub companies absorb some of the risk on behalf of the subcontractors (that is, $\alpha > 0$). Even more interesting, they also found that α grows, among other things, with the degree of risk aversion of the subcontractor and the size of the fluctuations in costs. In other words, large companies do take up on risk, if that is what the subcontractors need. Finally, they found an average α of 0.69, with many of the contracts having a factor above 0.75. This means that the contracts are closer to the cost-plus end of the spectrum.[10] This is, in fact, very close to what a working relationship *within a company* is.

The risk-sharing agreement is basic to the long-term success of the relationship, and the large company has to be willing to take risks. The supposed exploitation is certainly nowhere to be found. The arrangement gives flexibility to the large firm while the subcontractor is better off because of the risk absorbed by the big company, which is presumably more risk neutral, for its size allows it to absorb fluctuations.

Benetton is full of examples like this. Remember that it keeps in-house those knitting operations that require the use of over-specialized machinery, which runs a big risk of becoming obsolete overnight if fashion changes. It does not want a small subcontractor to be stuck with an investment it cannot use. For the large company, buying a few machines that cannot be used is not a big problem. For a small subcontractor, however, it could be devastating. It is efficient therefore for Benetton to take up that risk, and to subsidize its subcontractors if they ever get into this kind of trouble. This procedure is known throughout the system, and the trust it generates reinforces its efficiency, as we have seen.

From the point of view of the other members of the network, managing their business becomes somewhat different from managing a 'normal', 'stand alone' operation. They don't have to worry about getting clients (suppliers, in the case of downstream members of the network) but on adding as much value as possible to the system. Adaptation becomes the name of the game. How can my company make life easy for the rest of the network? The more successful a company becomes at that, the stronger its position within the network will be.

Many people feel that concentrating all one's energies on adding value to one client is a very risky position to be in. But it is not all that different from what most managers do: they devote all their effort and energy to be useful to just one company, for which they work full-time. They take such a 'risky' position (seen from a purely competitive point of view) for three reasons: first, as we saw, they realize they can make more money that way, because their full-time cooperation lets the company create more value than they would be able to create on their own; second, they expect the company will have some stability; and third, they know that whatever skills they develop working for the company should be marketable, with more or less effort, to another company, if the worst were to happen.

This is exactly the situation a member of a network is in. As we discussed at the beginning of this chapter, we simply must open up our field of vision, and let cooperative behaviour extend beyond the legal boundaries that define where a company ends and an 'outsider' starts. Thus instead of trying to balance risk by having as large a portfolio of clients as possible, a company may decide to concentrate on just one (two, at most), and do an outstanding job there. That is akin to the dictum: put all your eggs in *one* basket . . . and watch it carefully!

148

Conclusions

Strategic networks are long-term, purposeful arrangements among distinct but related for profit organizations that allow those firms in them to gain or sustain competitive advantage *vis-à-vis* their competitors outside the network, by optimizing activity costs and minimizing coordination costs. They do that because, in some industries, the best strategy is to coordinate in an adaptive fashion the whole business system, but doing it through vertical integration incurs heavy efficiency penalties.

Trust is at the very core of what a strategic network is, for it is the mechanism that lowers transaction costs, thus making the network viable economically.

Like any organizational form, it has its usefulness in specific areas. As we saw, those business systems that call simultaneously for close coordination and the maintenance of independent units are ripe for the network solution.

But like any organizational form it has its managerial requirements. From the point of view of the hub company, fostering trust and internalizing risk, so that reputation is not only preserved but constantly enhanced, is absolutely essential. From the other members of the network it is the constant effort to add value to the network (through adaptation, learning and diffusion of that learning) that will determine their future success.

In the next chapter, we shall analyse how these notions can be applied to international strategy. As we shall see, this is a paradoxical problem, for internationalization implies both excellent rewards and thorny problems for a networking solution.

References

1 The more conceptual aspects of this chapter draw heavily on some previous analyses, particularly J.C. Jarillo, 'On Strategic Networks', *Strategic Management Journal*, 1988, vol. 9, pp. 31–41; and J.C. Jarillo and J.E. Ricart, 'Sustain-

ing Networks', *Interfaces*, September–October 1987, pp. 82–91.

2 Michael Porter, *Competitive Strategy*, New York: The Free Press, 1980. See especially Chapter 1.

3 H.R. Coase, 'The Nature of the Firm', *Economica*, 4, 1937.

4 Oliver Williamson, following Coase's lead, called the two basic ways to coordinate economic activity 'markets' and 'hierarchies'. In the first we find arm's length relationships and prices as the coordinating device; in the second stable, hierarchical relationships and administrative 'fiat' as the coordinating mechanism. See Williamson, Oliver, *Market and Hierarchies*, New York: The Free Press, 1975.

5 See O. Williamsom, *op. cit.*

6 For a complete discussion of the concept of 'bounded rationality', see Simon, Herbert A., *Administrative Behavior*, New York: The Free Press, 1976.

7 H.B. Thorelli, 'Networks: Between markets and hierarchies', *Strategic Management Journal*, vol. 7, 1986, pp. 37–51.

8 Kreps has written extensively about why it is 'rational' in some circumstances not to be opportunistic, in order to preserve a reputation that creates more wealth than any possible misbehaviour. See, for instance, Kreps, D.M., *Game theory and economic modelling*, Oxford: Clarendon Press, 1991.

9 Axelrod, Robert, *The Evolution of Cooperation*, New York: Basic Books, 1984.

10 See S. Kawasaki and J. McMillan, 'The design of contracts: Evidence from Japanese subcontracting', Center for the Study of International Economic Relations Working Paper No. 8607C, Department of Economics, University of Western Ontario, London, Ontario, 1986.

7 International considerations

So far, very little mention has been made of geographic considerations. Besides mentioning that geographical proximity may be a positive factor when setting up a network, for it normally entails cultural proximity, we have been talking as if things happened in a geometric point, where distances or relative positions do not matter. But of course these things do matter: geographic considerations affect both the cost of the different activities and the cost of coordinating them.

International strategy deals with the geographic or spatial aspects of strategy. It is certainly beyond the scope of this book to deal with all the implications of international strategies, but a discussion of the main issues is necessary to complete the argument about coordination of the business system.[1]

To talk about the globalization of competition has become a cliché, but that does not make it less true. Figures 7.1 and 7.2

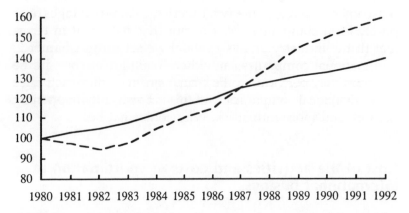

Figure 7.1 *Growth of world trade, compared to growth of the world's total population (1973 = 100)*

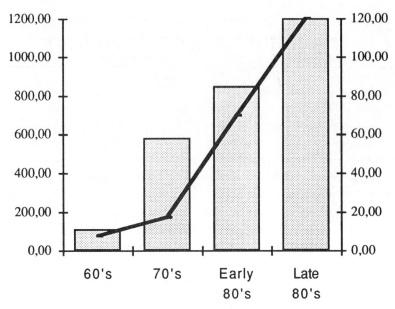

Figure 7.2   *Flows and accumulated foreign direct investment*

show some statistics, but dozens more could be added to show how more and more companies are selling their products on somebody else's markets, up to a point where 'international competition' is, in most industries, a matter of degree, always present to a some extent.

The underlying reason for this is that multinational companies do have, in many industries, clear advantages over purely local companies. We can put that statement in terms that fit the industry analysis model we set up in Chapter 2: multinational companies can either obtain lower costs in the activities they perform, or they can coordinate those activities better than local companies, and this is apparently happening in more and more industries. Why could that be?

Cost of the activities and costs of coordination in international business

First, it is well-known that some basic costs, such as labour, raw materials, or capital, vary widely among countries. Thus it is not surprising to find that those activities taking up a lot of direct labour, such as steelmaking or toy assembly, tend to be performed in countries where labour costs (adjusted for productivity, of course) are low. For the same reason aluminum is mostly smelted in those countries where electricity is cheap, such as Canada or France, for electricity makes up to a third of the cost of making aluminum. Economists call these differences in basic costs 'comparative advantages'. These advantages belong to countries rather than companies, and in principle any company operating in the country has access to that country's comparative advantages.

When those advantages are really important i.e. the cost differentials with the rest of the world are significant, multinational companies will dominate world markets, for only companies that perform the operation in the country or countries where the comparative advantages can be exploited will be competitive. This is true of basic commodities, such as oil exploration or tourism (dependent on sunshine), but also of more sophisticated 'inputs', e.g. it is not a coincidence that many high-tech industries tend to cluster in specific areas. They do so because conditions in those areas (the very presence of all the other companies) makes them attractive for business. For example, it is probably cheaper to set up a computer company in California than it would be in Zaire, for the basic inputs needed (engineers, suppliers) are much easier to come by in California.

Another reason why multinational companies may dominate local markets has already been discussed at length in Chapter 2, and that is economies of scale. If the minimum efficient scale to manufacture the tubes that are at the heart of colour TVs is several million per year, a company wanting to perform that activity efficiently must be international: purely local companies simply cannot compete, for there is no local market that can absorb the volume. Thus economies of scale, when they imply a large enough minimum efficient size, drive internationalization.

Economies of scale do not affect only manufacturing activity, as we saw in Chapter 2. Indeed it is one step earlier, in R&D, where the largest efficient scales are to be found. Thus a company may have to be international, i.e. sell in many countries, in order to amortize its expenditures in R&D, even if manufacturing can be done locally. This is, for instance, the case of many automobile companies; they have assembly plants in different countries, even when they are producing the same model. Again, this scale in R&D provides multinational companies with overwhelming competitive advantages over local ones, and it explains why whole industries, from computers to automobiles, from consumer electronics to pharmaceuticals, are completely dominated by a relatively small number of global players.

Of course reasons for 'playing it local' do exist. In many industries transportation costs more than offset any savings achievable through concentrated manufacturing. In other countries governments intervene heavily to protect local jobs and to force technology transfers. In yet others customers' demands vary by country, and standardizing global production, no matter how efficient, is not the best way to sell to them. For these reasons one finds many industries where not all activities in the business system can be performed either locally or globally: some activities are much more local than others. Sometimes the pros and cons of an international versus a local approach are fairly well balanced, and one finds companies pursuing different strategies (some local, some international) with comparable degrees of success. In fact most writings on international strategy are an attempt to shed light on how to deal with that tension, and they tend to recommend that the companies find their proper place, one that will be mostly determined by the nature of their industry, the countries they are already in, and their own 'administrative heritage', company culture and historical strengths.[2]

So much for activities, and how performing some of them efficiently may require crossing borders. But what about the other aspect, that of coordination? If some of the activities are to be performed internationally, while others are intrinsically local (think of selling to final customers!), then the coordination effort will also have to cross borders. This is by no means easy, and is by itself a crucial source of competitive advantage, even more so than it was in a purely local analysis, which we have been performing in the first part of the book. The impressive growth of international strategic alliances in the last few years[3] could be an indication of the felt need to coordinate the system more closely and, at the same time, of the difficulties companies find doing it on their own.

Thus, given a business system that calls for performing some of the activities internationally, companies playing in it will face the problem of coordinating internationally. As in the case of purely local systems, this can be done essentially in the three ways we know – by integrating vertically, by depending on the market, or by setting up a network. In the first case, the company becomes a 'fully fledged' multinational company, with subsidiaries in those countries where it operates. In the second, the company simply exports or imports those activities that have an international dimension, but it acquires very few assets or employees abroad, for it only engages in what can be done efficiently on a local basis. In the third case, of course, the company operates as though it were a multinational company, but relies on not-owned units for its international presence. An example will help us understand the logic behind each choice.

Vertical integration and subcontracting across borders

Take the case of Apple Computer. It has an assembly plant in Ireland, where it manufactures most of the computers it sells in Europe. It is evident that Apple's competitive advantage *vis-à-vis* European computer manufacturers cannot be in economies of scale in assembly, for it forgoes them by assembling separately in the US and in Europe. Its economies of scale are to be found upstream, in research and development, the activity that we called 'design' in Chapter 2.

But Apple does not have to assemble in Europe, with all the hassles that a foreign operation entails, to capture economies of scale in design. It could simply license its designs to a

European manufacturer, and reap the best of both worlds: high profits in the design activity, and 'European character' in the assembly activity, which might come as very useful when it comes to beating protectionism, getting Government orders or understanding local ways of doing business. Of course in Chapter 4 we saw why companies may not want to subcontract: the risks of poor coordination are clearly present. As a consequence, Apple decides to integrate foreign activities that could have been dealt with on a subcontracting basis. In so doing, it incurs all the important costs of running a multinational operation (logistic, coordinating, managerial, even political), but keeps its competitive edge.[4]

Economists have explained the existence of multinational companies that manufacture the same product in different countries along these lines, calling it the 'internalization theory'. It says that companies 'internalize' activities to be performed abroad i.e. integrate vertically across national borders, instead of relying on third parties, for a number of reasons. The most important ones come down to the general reasons we discussed in Chapter 4 on why relying on third parties may not be a good idea (opportunism, hollowing of the company), and they add one more reason: in many cases, the know-how that the company could transmit is not easy to price or even to transmit.[5]

For instance, Procter & Gamble is a successful American manufacturer and marketer of shampoo in Europe. To achieve that position, it replicates practically every activity of its business system in Europe. Competitive advantages *vis-à-vis* a local European competitor can only be found, then, on economies of scale in relatively basic R&D (the company routinely fine-tunes its formulae for European tastes and needs), and a superior marketing know-how. As is well known, Procter & Gamble has invented many features of modern consumer product marketing, such as brand management, market research, etc. Why doesn't P&G simply license its formulae and know-how, instead of replicating activities that are not a source of strong profits?

According to the internalization theory, the main reason is that the marketing know-how may be very difficult to price (how much is it really worth?), and simply impossible to transmit anyway. When the key to the success of an operation lies in the way the whole operation is managed, the only way to 'transfer' that knowledge may be simply to rebuild the whole operation from scratch. The only apparent exception is franchising, in which know-how can be priced (that is basically what the franchise fee pays for), and transferred: the franchiser's skill is in 'codifying' know-how in a way that can be precisely transferred. This works well in some industries, but would it be feasible for Procter & Gamble?

These natural difficulties to transfer know-how prevent the use of contractual arrangements – licenses, joint-ventures, strategic alliances – and other market-based forms.[6] Thus multinational companies integrate vertically across borders to avoid those difficulties. By dealing with internal units, a multinational company can protect its 'intangible assets', i.e. technology, patents, marketing know-how, etc., in the best possible way. Thus we could say, using the concepts developed in the book's first part, that it is the presence of transaction costs that drives companies to become multinational: they find that 'exporting' what they have to a third party would not work, and then decide to exploit it by integrating the foreign unit. Certainly the transaction costs of selling iron ore to a distant customer are very different from those Procter & Gamble would face if it tried to export its know-how. That's why many mining companies simply export (leave international coordination to the market), while other companies feel they must set up wholly owned and controlled subsidiaries. But, as we know, there is a third way to coordinate activities, one that is viable even when some of the coordination calls for specific assets and knowledge.

Think again of Benetton. As we know, the thousands of Benetton shops spread over the world are owned by independent operators. Benetton ships the merchandise direct from its warehouses in Northern Italy to each of the shops. It has practically no investment of any kind, not even for marketing purposes, in most of the countries where it operates: its external, exclusive agents take care of distribution and local coordination. Its standardized products and

157

approach to business are, moreover, strictly global: even its advertising is identical all over the world, always in English. Benetton certainly looks from outside like a typical multinational company, active in many countries.

But while the typical global multinational sells abroad through its own marketing organization, Benetton does it via external agents and franchised shops. However, Benetton's downstream operations (marketing and sales), although technically not part of the company, *are* an integral part of its strategy, as we know. One can look at Benetton as a purely exporting firm (which it, legally speaking, is), but it is probably more accurate to look at it as a truly multinational company, with a strong presence in many countries, even if the activities constituting such a presence (the shops and the country-based commercial organization) are not owned by Benetton. Thus it really coordinates its *worldwide* business system, for it needs the system in order to perform those activities it performs internally (purchasing, manufacturing planning) efficiently.

Even clearer would be the case of McDonald's. Again, strictly speaking, the company follows a strategy similar to a typical global company: very little foreign investment, with many activities concentrated in the home country, and high coordination among countries. This does not capture McDonald's real strategy, however: for all practical purposes – except legal – McDonald's *does* manufacture abroad, even if the operations are in the hands of franchisees. It does have a real presence in many countries, since most of the activities in its business system are performed locally. But they are not part of the company, in the sense of vertical integration. Thus international coordination is achieved through the network mechanism.

There are many other examples of companies that have a strong presence all over the world without internalizing all the activities of their business systems. Coca-Cola does not produce in most countries where it operates, but gives licences to local bottlers; and Holiday-Inn does not own many hotels abroad, but operates a lot via management contracts. So dismissing, by definition, a non-internalized activity as not the way a multinational company does things fails to capture the reality of its competitive strategy. Many companies keep (most) international activities external, yet are international in intent and scope.

International strategy: coordinating efficiently across borders

If we realize that, when going international, a company has exactly the same choices about how to coordinate the activities of its business system as when staying local, we must ask whether there is anything special about the whole issue of vertical integration when it is discussed across borders. The answer is yes.

Strategic alliances, or any use of external partners when going international, has generally been understood as a mechanism to lower the risk of entering an unfamiliar business territory, and that is surely the motivation in many cases. But, when that happens, we see the alliance as temporary – once the uncertainty disappears, the company will be ready to integrate the foreign unit. Indeed this is the way many companies have developed.[7] But using external partners may also be a (more permanent) optimal coordination strategy. Why? It can be argued that organization costs across borders tend to be higher than domestically – it is the traditional concept of 'the extra expense of doing business abroad'. Communications, transportation, monitoring, enforcement, etc., all tend to be more expensive compared to organizing a subsidiary in the home country. If this is the case, according to the preceding pages, firms will not internalize operations abroad and will rely on pure market mechanisms. This is shown by the fact that mechanisms such as licensing are more frequently used across borders than within the licenser's home country.[8]

But it can also be argued that transaction costs are also higher across borders. For a start, there is no superior authority to which one can effectively go in case of dispute. Often there are exclusivity clauses, needs to adapt the products or services to each country, high costs of information gathering, etc., with the result that the number of real available players is reduced, and creating specific assets may lead to opportunism. Again, according to the model, faced with such high costs, the firm will try to internalize. But if the costs of doing that are also high, the net result is that no transaction of any kind happens. In fact trade across borders is dramatically weaker than trade inside borders except for the smallest of countries: the USA exports and imports only about 10 per cent of its national product. Only a tiny minority of American companies do more business with the outside world (whose aggregate economy is three times as large as America's) than in their home country.

International business is in these circumstances less profitable than domestic business, and only firms with a very strong competitive advantage, i.e. high sustainable margins, can engage in it. As organization costs decrease, due to lower transportation and communications costs, for instance, more multinationalization (of the internal variety) can be expected. If transaction costs decrease, there should be more export activity, as now is happening within the European Community, where many companies are closing down foreign units and exporting from their home base. But, in any case, cooperation can reduce both costs, thus allowing a hitherto uneconomical transaction to take place.

Figure 7.3 summarizes the argument. If transaction costs are high and organization costs low, internalization, i.e. coordination through international vertical integration, takes place, provided there is some competitive advantage for the firm in the foreign country. If, on the contrary, organization costs are high and transaction costs low, a normal market-based relationship (export) takes place. But both costs can be high, in relative terms, across borders. In such circumstances, if there is no overwhelming competitive advantage, such as very large economies of scale, a transaction does not take place; or a mixed organizational form, one that lowers both costs, can arise, thus allowing the transaction to occur. Finally, if both transaction costs and organization costs are low, the theory leaves the question open: the final organizational form may simply depend on the company's historic position,[9] or

Integration costs

High   Low

		High	No transaction STRATEGIC NETWORK	SUBSIDIARY (INTEGRATION)
Transactions costs		Low	EXPORT (SUBCON- TRACTING)	INDIFFERENT

Figure 7.3 *Coordination choices according to the level of transaction costs and integration costs*

even custom, for companies may simply 'copy' what similar companies do.

Thus strategic networks may be an optimal organization mode also for international business, when both costs (internal organization and transactions) are especially high across borders, *and* there is an advantage to be had from coordinating worldwide operations closely. If not, international vertical integration, pure exporting, or simply staying local are more efficient solutions.

Conclusions

The internationalization of our economies is not going to stop increasing, regardless of some possible temporary protectionistic setbacks: the economic and political arguments are simply too strong to ignore. This will expose more and more companies to competition from companies they had never thought of as competitors before, and they will be forced to adapt to those newcomers. In many cases that adaptation will imply devising and implementing their own international strategy. For most companies internationalization will not be a choice, it will be really thrust upon them.

But the process of internationalization, or of managing an international company is an exceedingly difficult one. If we go back to the conceptualization of Chapter 2, we can say that international strategy is, first, the plan to locate given activities in particular locations and, second, the way to coordinate those activities around the world.

The two basic forms of coordination, however, have *added* problems when taken across borders. Thus a vertically integrated company has to deal with all the problems of vertical integration analysed in Chapter 3, plus the fact that the unit may be now thousands of kilometres away, managed by people from a different culture, playing to different environmental rules. The scope for asphyxiating bureaucracy is evident.

But arm's-length contracting may not be much better, for costs of international transactions tend to be higher than costs of national transactions. Often there is no clear legal authority to apply to, should things go awry. Cultural differences aggravate mistrust. Furthermore, financing an international deal (frequently done through irrevocable letters of credit) tends to be more expensive than financing national trade.[10]

At the same time, coordination needs may be higher, for there are more and more different parts to the system. Selling in different countries requires processing vast amounts of market information; and manufacturing in several countries may require complex logistics.

For all these reasons internationalization is more difficult than staying local. As a result, there is less international trade than it could be, and companies operating in large countries, such as the USA or Japan, have built-in advantages, for they can achieve respectable sizes before they encounter the extra complexities imposed by borders.

For all these reasons an international strategic network may be an excellent mode to organize international operations. In a way it is amazing the ease with which some of these networks (our well-known examples of Benetton or McDonald's come again to mind) have been able to transcend their borders, without losing any of their efficiency.

This way to coordinate may be crucial for small firms. Most

of them do not have the necessary resources to compete across the full spectrum of activities of their business system while obtaining the economies of scale necessary to remain competitive. The process of unification of European markets is leading to an increase in the minimum efficient scale, or so it is understood by companies.[11] This leaves them with a set of hard choices: facing the need to suddenly grow in size, they can either merge with other companies, preferably across borders (something very rarely achieved with a minimum of success); sell out to larger firms, thus becoming part of a vertically integrated system; or try to achieve the necessary scale by specializing in a few activities of the business system and then creating networking arrangements with foreign firms to take care of the rest.

In any case the conceptualization of joint ventures and other collaborative arrangements as a device to minimize transaction costs may throw light on a very common practice. Undoubtedly many international collaborative arrangements are started with different goals in mind, such as learning, capturing new skills, gaining easy access to new markets, or even just following a trend. But it is clear that in the long term only those arrangements that prove to be efficient will survive. If the motivations to start the venture are very different, its future will be doubtful: in fact, most joint ventures don't last long. But if, on the other hand, costs of internal organization and of transaction are minimized, i.e. if teaming up with another firm provides the advantages of integration and autonomy without raising the cost, then collaborative arrangements will become the cornerstone of a solid international strategy.

References

1 An earlier version of some of the ideas contained in this chapter can be found in J.C. Jarillo and J.I. Martínez, 'The International Expansion of Spanish Firms: Towards and Integrative Framework for International Strategy', in L.G. Mattsson and B. Stymne (eds), *Corporate and Industry Strategies for Europe: Adaptations to the European Single*

Market in a Global Industrial Environment, Amsterdam: North-Holland, 1990.

2 For an up-to-date analysis of the different problems facing multinational companies along these lines, and how to address them, see Bartlett, Christopher A. and Sumantra Ghoshal, *Managing Across Borders: The transnational solution*, Boston: Harvard Business School Press, 1989.

3 See, for instance, Hergert, Michael and Deigan Morris, 'Trends in International Collaborative Arrangements', in F.J. Contractor and P. Lorange (eds), *Cooperative Strategies in International Business*, Lexington: Lexington Books, 1988, pp. 99–109.

4 For an up-to-date treatment that integrates the dilemmas of international coordination, local responsiveness, and degree of internalization, see Jon H. Dunning, *Multinational Enterprises and the Global Economy*, New York: Addison Wesley, 1993.

5 For an excellent summary of economic thinking on internationalization, see Richard E. Caves, *Multinational Enterprise and Economic Analysis*, Cambridge: Cambridge University Press, 1982.

6 See Rugman, A.M., Lecrew, D.J. and Booth, L.D., *International Business: Firm and Environment*, New York: McGraw-Hill, 1985.

7 See Johanson, John and Vahlne, J.E., 'The Internationalization Process of the Firm – A Model of Knowledge Development and Increasing Foreign Market Commitments', *Journal of International Business Studies*, vol. 8, 1977.

8 See Caves, R., Crookell, H. and Killing, J., 'The Imperfect Market for Technology Licenses', Harvard University mimeo, 1982.

9 Bartlett and Ghoshal, *op. cit.*, talk about a company's 'administrative heritage' as an important determinant of a company's competitive position.

10 I owe this insight on how to quantify the extra transaction cost in an international deal to Prof. Ahmet Aykaç, of IMD.

11 Jarillo, J.C. and Martínez, J.I., *op. cit.*

8 General conclusions

The last 25 years have seen a shift from emphasis on purely functional organizations, where the idea was to maximize efficiency through specialization, breaking down companies into small units that took care of a single aspect of the business, to more holistic organizations, where even lower-level units were integral parts of the system or a sub-system. We see that from the emergence of the position of 'product manager' many years ago to the current emphasis on concepts such as teamwork, flat hierarchies, empowerment, and so on. This makes sense, for the efficiency gains achieved through sheer specialization of units are easily dissipated by the difficulty of coordinating those highly specialized, partial-optimizer units.

But what is true inside a company is also true inside the whole business system: there is a need for both efficient performance of each activity and close coordination, also achieved efficiently, i.e. without a suffocating bureaucracy. This is the essence of a strategic network, and in this sense we could say it is no more but the logical extension of the move, started within companies, towards *simultaneously* better, more efficient coordination and more individual responsibility and freedom.

This mode of organizing the whole system, which combines close coordination with a high degree of individual responsibility is clearly superior to the previous ones in those cases where it can be applied. What is interesting is how it is being applied to more and more industries that had been organized in a more traditional fashion.

Take the furniture industry. Traditionally it has been organized along the lines of the market mechanism:

independent producers would sell through a complex distribution system of wholesalers and retailers, all operating at arm's-length from each other. Coordination costs are high: furniture is extremely expensive to store, and intermediary stocks must therefore be minimized. The way that is traditionally done is that one orders a piece of furniture at the shop, where there is one piece on display (or sometimes out of a catalogue), and the order is sent upstream for the piece to be assembled and shipped, which may well take several months. This very inefficient way to organize the system has forced fragmentation of the industry and relatively low profitability.

But some new players are changing the rules of the game. Ikea has found a way to organize the system that ensures economies of scale can be obtained in practically all activities. Obtaining them calls for really *managing* the whole system in a fully integrated fashion, but Ikea is of course doing it through subcontractors, with whom it keeps very close, long-term relationships. Once again, the most interesting part in Ikea's success is not that it has happened (that could be attributed to the creativity of its founder), but that it can be imitated: as in the case of Benetton, or McDonald's, the *organization mode* is spreading throughout the industry, because it is simply a superior way to do business in that industry.

Of course the model has to be adapted for each industry, or even different segments of the industry. Within the furniture industry, nobody has yet been able to do it in the key segment of office furniture, and yet it seems ripe for it. When selling to a large company for a new building, the furniture company must deliver a large amount of furniture and install it. Installation, i.e. assembling the furniture, has to be done on site (the furniture cannot be transported fully assembled), and, since it is an essentially labour intensive operation, takes a large part of value added (about 30 per cent of the whole system), and is not subject to economies of scale. Moreover, economics makes it logical that it be done by a local company: shipping the workers with the furniture to a distant place, perhaps in a different country, would be prohibitively expensive.

The industry has been organized therefore on a purely market basis. Some manufacturers have emerged as important, by exploiting economies of scale in design and manufacturing, but they have had to leave final assembly to local distributors. Those distributors, in their desire to increase their sales, would carry the lines of different manufacturers. In a way it is exactly the same system the general apparel industry follows.

But if a company, along the Benetton lines, were able to control the whole system without paying the immense efficiency penalties that vertical integration would entail, it would obtain impressive advantages. For starters, the sales effort would be better focused, for local distributors would be exclusive and therefore concentrated on the company's products. But even more important, assembly, which is a huge part of the cost and a determinant of client satisfaction, could be much better controlled and coordinated. Going to this form of organization will require breaking traditional patterns and convincing people that it is in their interest to work differently. But the handful of companies that are starting to experiment with the system are also starting to move ahead of their competitors.

In many industries, however, strategic networks will not prove to be the superior way. Or they may be badly implemented. Consider the case of Coca-Cola. It has traditionally relied on local companies to do the bottling of its products, but in some cases those bottlers had squarely opposite interests. In the Philippines, for instance, the company with the exclusive bottling licence was also the country's largest brewer, and it was not surprising that beer (where the bottler had a better margin) was much more popular than Coke! But once those problems were ironed out, the system worked, to the extent that Coca-Cola is now using some of its best bottlers worldwide to take care of entering the newly opened Eastern European markets. In any case, when an industry meets the basic conditions to make it amenable for a strategic network, as we discussed in Chapter 6, someone has still to discover how to adjust the system to the specificities of the industry: its technology, underlying profits potential, opportunities for innovation, etc. But once (and if) that is done, both the 'inventor' and the early adopters stand to reap impressive benefits.

It is legitimate to ask, after reading the success stories mentioned in this book, what will the future bring. It is not difficult to see that a strategic network, based on trust and the 'fair sharing' of the pie, is much easier to manage when the pie is growing. What will happen to Benetton if (when) a downturn of the industry hits it?

The question is clearly important, but its implicit criticism of the network mechanism (it only works in good times, and when things go bad is everybody for himself) fails to see the deep advantages of the system. In effect a downturn in sales is certainly bad for the network, but would it be any better for an integrated company? A network is probably much more able to absorb downturns that either an integrated company or a purely market-based system. Think again of Benetton. If a general recession pulls down shops' sales by 15 per cent, shop owners (and, if it lasts long enough, manufacturing subcontractors) will go through a period of diminished profits or even some losses. This is fine, because that is exactly what a recession is supposed to do. An integrated company does not have that mechanism: one cannot reduce salaries easily, let alone stop paying them altogether! The network simply reflects external conditions much faster, which is what a 'good' organization is supposed to do. It is important anyway for would-be networkers to realize that it is precisely in bad times that strong links are forged, and that the treatment of the weaker parts of the network will certainly have a huge impact in the future level of trust, and with it the eventual efficiency of the whole system, as we have seen.

There is no question that the larger members of the network can take advantage of the small ones. We saw that in the analysis of the American auto companies' handling of their subcontractors. The question is whether doing that is efficient in the long run. I hope I've provided ample evidence in the book that by squeezing the weaker players, the strong ones may be simply introducing a level of extra costs in the system, which make them vulnerable to a new player that is not incurring those costs.

The last point in assessing the future potential of strategic networks as a mode of industry-wide organization has to do with social and economic trends. As more and more people become well educated and obtain a good standard of living, the desire for independence clearly grows. An organization based on smaller, more entrepreneurial units clearly fits the technological and social conditions of the twenty-first century better than the large monoliths prevalent in the last 100 years. The fact that the basic manufacturing activities are fast becoming less critical than the accompanying service also points in the same direction: efficient, prompt service calls for individually responsible units, not for large, bureaucratic hierarchies. The trend is accelerating. Companies such as Benetton are pushing ahead their relentless integration of the business system. Benetton has now started publishing its own general-interest magazine, because it does not like its advertising placed in magazines where it cannot really control the context. Not even Henry Ford would have gone for that level of integration! But Benetton of course is not publishing the magazine; a wholly committed subcontractor is doing it for them. As time passes, we are going to see more and more of this simultaneous tightening of coordination and vertical dis-integration that only strategic networks can provide.

International considerations must also be taken into account. Successful networking requires a specific frame of mind that is more germane in some cultures than others. In general, Anglo-Saxon business practices are much more individualistic, open, and market-based than are those of Japan or Continental Europe. One English manager in a transportation company referred to how difficult it was getting work from Japanese manufacturers in England by saying that, with their traditional suppliers, 'They have no contracts, only working relationships!' This cultural differences will be slowly smoothed out by the eventual success of the formula, although we should expect each company to implement it according to its own background.

I would like to finish these pages with a note of caution. In effect, all this discussion has been a gross simplification of reality. There are not just three ways to organize a business system, there is an infinite number. I've just painted *some* basic differences, trying to highlight *some* of the characteristics that differentiate *some* ways of doing business from others. To do that, I've had to put the emphasis on contradicting the more conventional ideas. But this does not mean I see strategic networks as *the* way to do things. In many cases there are more appropriate ways of doing business, and in all cases reality is a combination of all modes. But if my ideas help the reader think in more detail about coordination costs, about the advantages of closely integrating operations, about the fact that cooperation may be achieved not only though vertical integration, that bureaucracy can be eliminated by other ways than simple subcontracting, and that trust and long-term relationships may play an essential role in building competitive advantage in the real world, then the book will have fulfilled its purpose.

Bibliography

Anderson, E. and H. Gatignon, 'Modes of Foreign Entry: A Transaction Cost Analysis and Propositions'. *Journal of International Business Studies*, Vol. 17, 1986.

Andrews, Kenneth R., *The Concept of Corporate Strategy*, New York: Dow Jones-Irwin, 1971.

Axelrod, Robert, *The Evolution of Cooperation*, New York: Basic Books, 1984.

Bain, Joseph, *Industrial Organization*, New York: Wiley and Sons, 1959.

Bartlett, Christopher A. and Sumantra Ghoshal, *Managing Across Borders: The transnational solution*, Boston: Harvard Business School Press, 1989.

Boscheck, Ralf, 'Tetra-Pak', IMD case, 1992.

Caves, Richard E., *Multinational Enterprise and Economic Analysis*, Cambridge: Cambridge University Press, 1982.

Caves, R., H. Crookell, and J. Killing, 'The Imperfect Market for Technology Licenses', Harvard University mimeo, 1982.

Chandler, Alfred: *Strategy and Structure: Chapters in the History of the American Industrial Enterprise*, Cambridge, Mass.: The MIT Press, 1962.

Clark, Kim and Takahiro Fujimoto, *Product Development Performance*, Harvard Business School Press, Boston: 1991.

Coase, Ronald H., 'The Nature of the Firm', *Economica*, vol. 4, 1937.

Contractor, Farok J. and Peter Lorange (eds), *Cooperative Strategies in International Business*, Lexington: Lexington Books, 1988.

Dunning, Jon H., *Multinational Enterprises and the Global Economy*, New York: Addison Wesley, 1993.

Gilbert, Xavier and Paul Strebel, 'Developing Competitive Advantage', in H. Mintzberg (ed.), *The Strategy Process*, Englewood Cliffs, New Jersey: Prentice-Hall, 1987.

Hergert, Michael and Deigan Morris, 'Trends in International Collaborative Arrangements', in F.J. Contractor and P. Lorange (eds), Cooperative Strategies in International Business, Lexington: Lexington Books, 1988.

Jarillo, J. Carlos, 'On Strategic Networks', *Strategic Management Journal*, vol.9, 1988.

Jarillo, J. Carlos and Jon I. Martínez, 'Benetton S.p.A.', Harvard Business School case #9–389–074, 1988.

Jarillo, J.C. and J.I. Martínez, 'The International Expansion of Spanish Firms: Towards and Integrative Framework for International Strategy', in L.G. Mattsson and B. Stymne (eds), *Corporate and Industry Strategies for Europe: Adaptations to the European Single Market in a Global Industrial Environment*, Amsterdam: North-Holland.

Jarillo, J. Carlos and Joan E. Ricart, 'Sustaining Networks', *Interfaces*, September–October 1987.

Jarillo, J. Carlos and Howard H. Stevenson, 'Co-operative strategies: the payoffs and the pitfalls', *Long Range Planning*, vol. 24. No.1, 1991.

Johanson, John and J.E. Vahlne, 'The Internationalization Process of the Firm – A Model of Knowledge Development and Increasing Foreign Market Commitments', *Journal of International Business Studies*, vol. 8, 1977.

Kawasaki, S. and J. McMillan, 'The design of contracts: Evidence from Japanese subcontracting', London, Ontario: Center for the Study of International Economic Relations Working Paper No. 8607C, Department of Economics, University of Western Ontario, 1986.

Kay, John, *Foundations of Corporate Success*, Oxford: Oxford University Press, 1993.

Kreps, D.M., *Game theory and economic modelling*, Oxford: Clarendon Press, 1991.

Lorenzoni, Gianni, 'From Vertical Integration to Vertical Disintegration', paper presented at the Strategic Management Society Conference, Montreal, 1982.

Magaziner, Ira C. and Mark Patinkin 'Fast Heat: How Korea

Won the Microwave War', *Harvard Business Review*, January–February 1989.

Pastin, Mark, 'The Hollow Corporation', *Executive Excellence*, vol. 5, 1988.

Porter, Michael E., *Competitive Strategy*, New York: The Free Press, 1980.

Porter, Michael E., 'The contributions of industrial organization to strategic management', *Academy of Management Review*, vol. 6, no. 4, 1981.

Porter, Michael E., *Competitive Advantage*, New York: The Free Press, 1985.

Porter, Michael E., *The competitive advantage of nations*, New York: The Free Press, 1990.

Prahalad, C.K. and Gary Hammel, 'The Core Competences of the Corporation', *Harvard Business Review*, May–June 1990.

Rappaport, Andrew S. and Halevi Shmuel, 'The Computerless Computer Company', *Harvard Business Review*, July–August, 1991.

Rugman, A.M., D.J. Lecraw, and L.D. Booth, *International Business: Firm and Environment*, New York: McGraw-Hill, 1985.

Servan-Schreiber, Jean-Jacques, *The American Challenge*, Avon, 1965.

Shelton, John, 'Allocative Efficiency vs X-Efficiency: Comment', *American Economic Review*, vol. 57, 1967.

Simon, Herbert A., *Administrative Behavior*, New York: The Free Press, 1976.

Thorelli, H.B., 'Networks: Between markets and hierarchies', *Strategic Management Journal*, vol. 7, 1986.

Von Hippel, Erik: *User Innovation: An analysis of the functional sources of innovation*, Cambridge, Mass: Sloan School of Management, Massachusetts Institute of Technology, 1985.

Williamson, Oliver, *Market and Hierarchies: Analysis and Antitrust Implications*, New York: The Free Press, 1975.

Womack, James P., Daniel T. Jones, and Daniel Roos, *The Machine That Changed The World*, New York: Rawson Associates, 1990.

Index